Calypso Rose

THE CARIBBEAN BIOGRAPHY SERIES

The Caribbean Biography Series from the University of the West Indies Press celebrates and memorializes the architects of Caribbean culture. The series aims to introduce general readers to those individuals who have made sterling contributions to the region in their chosen field – literature, the arts, politics, sports – and are the shapers and bearers of Caribbean identity.

Series Editor: Korah Belgrave

Other Titles in This Series

Earl Lovelace, by Funso Aiyejina
Derek Walcott, by Edward Baugh
Marcus Garvey, by Rupert Lewis
Beryl McBurnie, by Judy Raymond
Una Marson, by Lisa Tomlinson
Stuart Hall, by Annie Paul
Lucille Mathurin Mair, by Verene Shepherd
Aimé Césaire, by Elizabeth Walcott-Hackshaw
Walter Rodney, by Rupert Lewis
Richie Richardson, by Densil A. Williams

CALYPSO ROSE

Gelien Matthews

The University of the West Indies Press
Mona · St Augustine · Cave Hill · Global · Five Islands

The University of the West Indies Press
7A Gibraltar Hall Road, Mona
Kingston 7, Jamaica
www.uwipress.com

© 2026 by Gelien Matthews
All rights reserved. Published 2026

A catalogue record of this book is
available from the National Library of Jamaica.

ISBN: 978-976-658-031-5 (pbk)
978-976-658-030-8 (hbk)
978-976-658-032-2 (ePub)

Cover/Jacket and book design by Robert Harris
Cover photograph by Richard Holder
Set in Whitman 11.5/15

Printed in the United States of America

CONTENTS

ONE / 1

TWO / 18

THREE / 33

FOUR / 49

FIVE / 68

SIX / 82

NOTES / 93

BIBLIOGRAPHY / 101

ACKNOWLEDGEMENTS / 111

ONE

McCartha Linda Monica Sandy-Lewis, popularly known in the calypso world as Calypso Rose or Rose, is a celebrated musical icon with an excellent local and international profile. She was born on 27 April 1940 in the village of Bethel in Tobago, the sister isle of the twin-island Republic of Trinidad and Tobago. Her first name, McCartha, grew out of her mother's intuition that, despite her unassuming physical appearance as a child, her daughter possessed superior potential that was destined to be realized. Rose herself admitted that as an infant, she was a sorry sight. She was thin, sucked her middle finger, had very short hair and spoke with a stammer.[1] In her mother's heart, nevertheless, her fourth child, just like Douglas MacArthur, the American general of the US army during World War II, was born for greatness. Thus, she named her after General MacArthur. The battles Rose fought and won throughout her life justify the weighty name her mother chose for her.

Not much is known about Rose's mother. The calypsonian has made strenuous efforts to keep her personal life out of the public domain. It is known, however, that her mother's name was Dorchea Sandy, a migrant from Grenada to Tobago.[2] Her maiden name was Ford.[3] She must have been physically robust, for she produced thirteen offspring, eleven of whom survived childhood. Eight of the surviving children were girls, and three were boys. Apart from Rose, the name of only one other daughter is known. The *Trinidad Express* reported in 2000 that Jean Sandy, Rose's sister, received the Humming Bird Gold Medal on the calypsonian's behalf from President A. N. R. Robinson.[4] Rose often mentions her three brothers, the third, fifth and sixth children of her mother; Kelvin, Sonny and Lloyd.[5] The calypsonian fondly remembers fighting with these boys as a child while living with them in Tobago. She has also indicated that her brother Lloyd became a herbalist from whom she obtained "bush medicine" so helpful in treating her battle with gout.[6] These three boys, in time, all migrated to New York. Their mother was a religious woman who faithfully attended the Baptist Church in L'Anse Fourmi each Sunday with her husband and many children.

A little more is known about Rose's father than about her mother. His name was Altino Sandy, a migrant from Happy Hill, Grenada.[7] In Tobago, he developed a reputation as a strong-willed and independent individual. He was popularly known in his role as a Spiritual or Shouter Baptist minister. He had his own church in L'Anse Fourmi, and although he was semi-literate, he excelled at preaching.[8] Rose recollects that her father was ultra-religious. His spiritual beliefs influenced every choice he made and every action he took. Under his roof, his children did not use their free time listening to music on the

ONE

radio or participating in other activities which he considered "worldly". In fact, in her first home, there was neither electricity nor musical appliances.[9] Family members could not even whistle in Altino Sandy's house. Attendance at church and involvement in its activities were primarily the extent of his wife and children's social experiences. Rose also remembers that every service her father led began with the spiritual "By the Rivers of Babylon".[10] Thus, when his daughter became a calypsonian, not only did he condemn the genre as devil music but also wondered where she had taken up the "vice", since no such melodies were tolerated under his roof. Altino Sandy, by occupation, was also an independent fisherman. He had two boats and conducted his self-employed business in the Mount Ville Bay area in Tobago.

Rose's love for and strong attachment to the sea have been influenced by her fisherman father, whom she often accompanied to the ocean each morning while still living with him in Tobago. Rose professes a love for all kinds of seafood and is fully convinced of their nutritious and healing properties. She also testifies about the therapeutic value of sea bathing. There is a counter-narrative about Altino Sandy that is not widely repeated. Newspaper writer Simon Lee describes Rose's father as a village ramgoat or philanderer of Bethel, Tobago. He was a fisher not only of souls but also of women, for while he sired thirteen children with his lawfully wedded wife, he had seven other children with other women.[11] Altino Sandy's extramarital affairs were contrary to his profession as a spiritual leader and hardly qualified him to condemn his daughter's chosen career.

Rose traces her family in Tobago back to her maternal great-grandmother, Martha Paul. In one of her calypso compositions, entitled "Back to Africa", Rose reminisces about the first six years of her life, when her great-grandmother was alive. Paul was captured in Guinea and forcibly transported across the Atlantic to the Americas, where she was subjected to servile labour. She eventually settled in Mt Irvine Bay, Tobago. Rose recalls that her great-grandmother was a very tall, thin woman with long ears. She smoked tobacco using a charcoal pipe and, particularly in her last days, often stooped to the ground and gazed at the sea, no doubt trying to reconnect with the African homeland from which she was forcefully removed and for which she retained to the end of her days a great longing to be reunited. Rose remembers her saying, "Pickney, no man know dey burial ground".[12] Rose explains that this meant that no one knows where they would be buried when death comes. Rose notes that Martha Paul, a slave name, was of the Ibo tribe who, because of her capture, was denied the right to be buried in her ancestral homeland. Her great-grandmother's direct connection with Africa has been a continual muse for the calypsonian. Rose says about her great-grandmother, "I remember her and her stories".[13] Martha Paul has served as a vital link to Rose's connections to her African ancestry and sense of identity, both of which feature in her music. Rose also claims that her great-great-great-grandfather was Sandy, the leader of the first, largest and most successful rebellion of the enslaved in Tobago.[14] In Sandy's Revolt of 1770, the black freedom fighters succeeded in seizing arms and ammunition stored at Fort James in Plymouth, destroying by fire the Great

ONE

House of the Mt Irvine Bay Sugar Plantation and killing its proprietor, Samuel Hall and eleven other white persons.[15] The relationship Rose establishes between herself and Sandy, the black revolutionary, underscores her claim to a family history marked by black power and resistance.

One of Rose's grandfathers was a musical master. He was both an instrumentalist and a vocalist. He played the fiddle and was often commissioned to sing at weddings and other social gatherings in Tobago. He was also well known in his village community as a member of one of Tobago's popular speech bands. Rose points out that the speech bands were integral to old-time Carnival celebrations in Tobago. The speech "banddist", as Rose calls her grandfather, would compose lyrics on the spot on any subject.[16] The audience would be wildly entertained by these witty, spontaneously composed oral renditions in the same way that audiences are delighted by the ingenuity of "extempo" calypsonians or free-style rappers. Rose also remembers that her grandfather and other members of speech bands in Tobago would imitate historical figures such as Sir Walter Raleigh, not only in their speeches but also in their attire. They were particularly fond of wearing the extravagant hats of the European sailors. Another musical giant in Rose's family tree was a grandmother who was also a member of the Spiritual Baptist faith. She was a singer. Rose also boasts of a great-uncle who sang in several choirs in Tobago. The roots of her talent as a writer, singer, entertainer and activist can be traced to several elders in Rose's Tobago family, including her Baptist minister father.[17]

Rose admits that growing up in Tobago as a child with many siblings, a semi-literate, self-employed father and living in a small two-bedroom house in a rural fishing village was financially challenging. Ultimately, economic hardship prompted her migration from Tobago to Trinidad.

Rose was informally adopted by her father's brother, Aleto Sandy, who lived at Twelfth Street, Barataria, Trinidad. He had no children of his own and was willing to help his brother, who had responsibility for feeding a large family.[18] Dorchea and Altino Sandy were relieved by the offer of assistance and fully cooperated with the arrangement. From the young age of nine, Rose's world shifted from Tobago to Trinidad. Uncle Sandy was a fundamental Seventh-day Adventist. While he agreed to take charge of Rose's material upkeep, he was not very involved in the child's socialization. This task, he entrusted to his common-law wife, Edith Robinson, Aunt Robbie. Rose regarded Edith Robinson both as an aunt and a mother who treated her well and showed her love. In her recollections, she declares that Aunt Robbie was a Baptist Christian who was flexible enough to enjoy the pleasures of this world. She loved to cook and was a party girl. More significantly, Rose credits Aunt Robbie as the woman who nurtured her talent as a calypsonian. Soon after she arrived in Trinidad, Aunt Robbie enrolled Rose in the San Juan Anglican Primary School located on Second Street in Barataria. Rose remembers being bullied during the day at school because of her stammering problem and her country ways and appearance, but comforted by her adopted mother at home in the evening. In time, the shy girl from Tobago

ONE

blossomed into a local schoolgirl star. She explains the role Aunt Robbie played in her metamorphosis:

> My auntie, she had all the calypso records. She would grind up the gramophone and tell me, "Dance, dance, dance!" On Sunday night, she'd take me down to the clubs where they would be singing and moving until Monday morning, oh my God, it was fantastic! I was on the roof! My auntie would be wearing her shorts, and we were all just wiggling the bamsee [bottom] left-right, left-right.[19]

Soon after settling in Trinidad, Rose was composing calypsos, singing in the school choir and at weddings, christenings and other social gatherings in the community. By age fifteen, in 1955, having been introduced by Aunt Robbie to the nightclubs in and around Port of Spain, McCartha became a regular feature of the Original Young Brigade Calypso Tent led by calypsonian Spoiler, whose birth name was Theophilus Philip. Embracing the tradition among the calypso fraternity of adopting a stage sobriquet, she initially called herself Crusoe Kid. She was from Tobago, an island associated with the Robinson Crusoe legend. Spoiler rejected the Crusoe nickname. Mindful of the fact that, as a woman, she was a pioneer who could pave the way for other women to be accepted in this otherwise male-dominated arena, Spoiler offered her the stage name Calypso Rose.[20] He explained that while there were one or two other women who at that time were singing calypso, she could become, like the mother of all flowers, the rose, the mother of calypso, the woman who could break the stranglehold men exerted over calypso. Rose was delighted with the ascription and has since proudly and effectively embodied it.

In 1963, Rose made her first trip to perform outside of Trinidad and Tobago. She participated in the Calypso King competitions in both Grenada and St Thomas. It was a history-making experience. Rose emerged as the winner of the Road March and Calypso King competitions held in St Thomas in 1963 with her rendition of "Cooperation". The composition was a plea to Carnival revellers to eliminate violence from the street festival. Rose amusingly reflects on this victory, noting that she was the first woman to become a king.[21] Like many other calypsonians from Trinidad in the second half of the twentieth century, Rose became a regular performer at the Virgin Islands Carnival celebrations held in April.[22] The first of this tour, the 1963 event, was organized by a promoter from Guyana, Mr Cyril Shaw. He recruited calypsonians Cristo, Blakie, King Short Shirt, King Obstinate and the only female in the cast, Calypso Rose.[23] It was during her frequent visits to the Virgin Islands in the 1960s and 1970s that Rose took a husband. In several interviews retracing her life, Rose claimed that her name changed from Sandy to Sandy Lewis when she married Aubrey Lewis in 1966.[24] The marriage ceremony was performed in the US Virgin Islands. While still a young woman, Rose declared that she would never marry a Tobagonian since they were all related. She explained that the Sandys of Plymouth, the Charles of L'Anse Fourmi and the Denoons and Pauls of Canaan, Bon Accord and Speyside were all connected by blood.[25] Very little is known about her husband and their relationship, except that the marriage ended in 1983. In her interview with Rudolph Ottley, Rose revealed that her husband died on 12 January 1983, the beginning of her widowhood.[26] It is interesting to note, however, that in the trailer to the documentary entitled *Lioness of the Jungle*, Rose declares that "I have never been to bed with a man since I was raped to now because I'm still afraid."[27] Rose became a victim of rape at the age of eighteen, and she was already twenty-three when her marriage to Aubrey Lewis took place. These demographic details, along with her admission about her relationship with men, suggest that her marriage to Lewis may not have been consummated.

Soon after Rose won the Calypso Monarch competition, she set her sights on migration, with the aim of becoming a cultural ambassador on the international stage for the indigenous music of Trinidad and Tobago. The immediate cause of her decision to relocate from Trinidad and Tobago, however, was scandalous in nature. Rose recalled visiting the Foreign Exchange Counter of the Central Bank of Trinidad and Tobago in 1986 to purchase US$100. To her chagrin, she waited for service almost the entire day and at 3:45 p.m., just fifteen minutes before closure, the clerk informed her that she had to declare her assets before the foreign exchange transaction could be approved. True to her feisty nature, Rose responded that as a holder of a Trinidad and Tobago passport, she should not be subjected to such shoddy treatment and that she had already declared her assets in San Juan, Trinidad, and in Tobago. In a tone that Rose considered very rude, the clerk finally said to her, "Take yuh money and go."[28] Rose felt slighted by the incident, which occurred when the People's National Movement (PNM), led by Patrick Manning, was in power. She turned her back on the

PNM, and by 1983, she made Queens, New York, her adopted home. In the early years of Rose's migration to New York, she embarked on studies which departed significantly from her career as a calypso entertainer. She studied criminology. Rose states that her motivation for studying criminology was her long-standing love of law. No wonder, then, that in 1974 she released a number entitled "Constable Rose". In the calypso, she expresses a serious intention to clear the capital city of Port of Spain, of violence and unsavoury behaviour. She vows to enforce the full extent of the law on gamblers, drug addicts, loiterers, gun-toting members of gangs and prostitutes, all of whom she intends to lock up.[29] Rose's first module in the field of criminology was a home study course in fingerprinting, which she took in the late 1960s, even before she migrated to the United States of America. By the time she moved to New York, the range of legal courses she pursued included security, industrial espionage, fire control, narcotics, types of evidence and surveillance. Among her teachers was a former Central Intelligence Agency operative.[30] Having completed the Auxiliary Police Primary Training Course Class 82 – Q – 16 in 1982,[31] Rose served as an auxiliary police officer on Queens Boulevard, New York, until 1985. She was a reserve volunteer. Her duties in this post primarily involved community policing and engagement with local neighbourhoods.[32] For example, the post required Rose to carry a firearm, manage crowd control at special events, perform traffic control during accidents and emergencies, assist with sobriety checkpoints and report on hazardous conditions.[33] Rose's foray into legal affairs, however, was short-lived. She resigned from the New York Police

Department (NYPD) following a bout of illness. Rose recalls, however, that her law enforcement certification led Prime Minister Eric Williams and Police Commissioner Randolph Burrows to offer her positions in the Central Intelligence Department (CID) of Trinidad and Tobago in the late 1980s. She explains that she did not accept these offers because "I felt I would be stationary and wouldn't be able to sell the country as I have been doing, and besides, I love Calypso . . . I haven't regretted being who I am and what I am."[34] She also admits that "I liked the field [criminology], but I love entertainment more."[35] Rose's brief sojourn into police work in New York did not supplant her love for composing and performing on the calypso stage.

Rose never made Belize her home, but the calypsonian has a special, intimate connection to this country. Her close association with Belize began soon after she won her first Road March title in Trinidad in 1977, when she sang "Gimme More Tempo", also known as "Tempo" and "Going Down San Fernando". Rose recalls that in the season following this victory, the then minister of culture of Belize, Mr Henry Young, invited her to entertain in several shows leading up to the country's Independence Day celebration, which takes place on 30 September each year. Rose notes that she was warmly received on her first visit, which led to subsequent unbroken appearances each year in early September from 1978 to 1983. Rose also remembers her introduction to the Garifuna culture of the First Peoples of Belize in the area known as Gangriga. Her exposure to the Garifuna music and dance, known as punta, fired her imagination and motivated her to write and perform two calypsos to honour and promote Belizean culture. The first calypso was entitled "Leh We Punta". It highlighted Garifuna punta music, drumming, dancing, drinking and villages like Gangriga. The second was "Fire in Belize", a calypso promoting the modern revival of September Carnival in Belize. The people of Belize enthusiastically received the two compositions and are among Rose's more popular calypsos. Another reason why Belize is home away from home for Rose is that her resurgence following the release of her 2016 album *Far from Home* was, in great measure, facilitated by her collaboration with Belizeans in the music industry. The producer of the album, Ivan Duran, is from Belize. Several of the musicians accompanying the vocalists are also from Belize, and the label Stonetree is Belizean.[36] Belize, as well as France, as shall be examined shortly, was intimately connected with Rose's development, especially in the latter part of her long and successful career. In recognition of her regional and international promotion of Belize's music and culture, the government made her an honorary Belizean.[37]

Rose is a globetrotter who has performed on almost every continent, gracing the stages of countries such as Morocco, Italy, Nigeria, Canada, Japan and Malaysia, to name a few. Trinidad-based *Newsday* reporter Joan Rampersad reported that in 2017 alone, Rose performed ninety-eight sold-out shows in Europe and North America.[38] In 2019, Rose made history when she became the oldest performer at age seventy-eight to perform at Coachella. This music and art festival, held each April in California, is a grand extravaganza showcasing the musical talent of the world's best performers. While a few other

ONE

calypsonians, namely Machel Montano, Bunji Galin and Fay Anne Lyons starred previously at Coachella, Rose was the first and, to date, the only calypso singer to be given a full set totalling forty-five minutes on that world stage. At Coachella 2019, Rose's name appeared on billboards alongside other internationally famous musical artistes such as Ariana Grande, Janelle Monae, Whiz Khalifa and DJ Khaled.[39] Other North American, African and European concerts in which Rose has been booked include the Montreux Jazz Festival in Switzerland, the World Music Festival in Chicago, the Africa Festival in Würzburg, the WOMAD Festival in England, Couleur Café and the Brussels Summer Festival in Belgium, Pohoda in Slovakia and the Roskilde Festival in Denmark. Rose's repeat appearances at music festivals around the world are a testament to the timeless nature of her music and her universal appeal.

Notwithstanding the wide geographic spread of her performances, no other country outside of the Americas has been home away from home for Rose more than France. One scholar who has followed Rose's career in France is Dr Andil Gosine[40] of York University in Toronto. Gosine observes that the album that announced to the world Rose's close association with France was *Far from Home*, first released in 2016. By the time the album hit the airwaves, the French media, the music industry, and the public at large were already enraptured by the music of the Tobago-born calypsonian. The album was a bestseller in France, featuring hits such as "Leave Me Alone", "I Am African" and "Abatina". It reached the top ten in the French pop charts and went on to be certified gold (sold five hundred thousand copies). Sales continued to mount, bringing the album to platinum status (sales surpassed five hundred thousand copies), a rare achievement for calypso on the world music market. The demand for this album in France and around the world has been so overwhelming that three versions have been produced. The deluxe re-edition of 2017, with added tracks, followed the first release in 2016. Continued demand led to the production of the third version. The climax of the French embrace of Rose occurred on the night of 11 February 2017, when she became the recipient of the Victoires de la Musique Prize, more commonly known as the French Grammys, for Best Music Album. This was a mammoth achievement. It marked a resurgence in her career when she was seventy-six years, going on seventy-seven, an age when many entertainers are well into retirement. It was also a measure of the depth and breadth of her popularity. The unassuming girl from Tobago rose above other international musical giants who perform a multiplicity of genres known collectively as world music. Gosine declares that Rose's success and critical acclaim in France are not surprising. He points out that by the turn of the new millennium, the French appreciation for world music, and more particularly for the music of the Global South, was well established. One of Paris' most popular radio stations, Top 40 Radio, churns out a wide variety of musical genres, including calypso, reggae, the blues and pop from artists such as Britney Spears from the United States, Natasha Atlas from Ethiopia, Lara Fabian from France and Youssou N'Dour from Senegal. France is currently the top per capita consumer of global music. Gosine posits that Rose won the hearts of the French because France, in general and Paris in particular, more than any

ONE

other city in the world, embraces all types of music originating from the Global South. On another note, Gosine appropriately asserts that France's enthusiastic embrace of Rose, a former colonized member of the French Caribbean empire, emerges from both a guilty and a nostalgic consciousness that seeks to recompense, on the one hand, the wrongs of colonial rule and, on the other hand, to continue extending paternalism. The colonial theme in Rose's association with the French was not lost on the calypsonian, who, in her acceptance speech on the night of the Victoires de la Musique award ceremony, was mindful to point out that her great-grandmother, Martha Paul, was a captive from French Guinea.[41] Rose's comment was a not-so-subtle reminder of the culpability of France in the trans-Atlantic slave trade, slavery and colonial rule. Gosine also credits Rose's now-former manager, the Frenchman Jean-Michel Gibert, as a huge influence on the calypsonian's belated renaissance in France. Gibert was the man, Gosine correctly asserts, who re-conceptualized Calypso Rose within French popular culture as a world music artist. In the four years that he managed her, Gibert introduced and promoted Rose in France and widened her international collaborations. The expanded network included the French and Spanish composer, producer and performer Manu Chao, who first visited Rose in Trinidad and Tobago during the 2012 Carnival season. Over the next four years, Chao, along with other musicians and producers such as Ivan Duran from Belize and the band Kobo Town from Toronto, worked with Rose to produce the 2016 album *Far from Home*, which manager Gibert promoted in France as well as in other European countries such as Germany, Belgium, Spain and

Switzerland.[42] The format of the promotion also went a long way toward integrating Rose into France. She became a regular feature of French media, appearing as a guest on the popular television programme *The Breakfast* as well as on night-time talk shows. Her manager also booked Rose to perform at several large entertainment venues in France, including the Olympia in Paris. While Gosine's analysis of Rose's connections to France is incisive, one dimension he overlooked is the infectious yet easy rhythm and catchy lyrics of her compositions. From the 1970s onwards, soca, an upbeat and fast-paced offshoot of calypso, became the rage. International audiences, however, tended to be put off by the frenetic pace and the difficult-to-follow, parochially based lyrics of soca. Rose, to her advantage, while experimenting with mixing her music with other genres such as reggae and soul, has remained true to the originally slower, more lyrically discernible calypso. This combination makes her music attractive and accessible to audiences in France and the wider world.[43] Rose also provides another incisive explanation for her belated popularity not just in France but on the European continent as a whole. Rose shared with Ottley in an interview that, for many years, Europeans have been tourists at the Trinidad and Tobago Carnival. When they return home, they carry souvenirs, including steel pans, calypso recordings, brochures and magazines covering Carnival activities. They keep some of the memorabilia for themselves and share others with friends and family. They thus become transmitters of the Carnival culture, preparing the ground for the concerts that Rose and other practitioners of the art form staged internationally.[44] Rose succeeded in infusing her career with

ONE

an incomparable level of longevity. This success was largely facilitated through her association with France.

From a little remote village in her Caribbean-island home not larger than twenty-five miles long and six miles wide, Rose successfully traversed national, regional and international borders to become a global star known and celebrated by hundreds of thousands at home and abroad.

TWO

Calypso Rose could not have imagined back in the 1950s when she first entered the calypso tent that her musical career would be as successful as it proved to be. For much of the twentieth century, calypso was a man's world, and women who attempted to break through its gender barriers faced serious opposition. The profession itself was portrayed as one that was hypersexual and masochistic. It was not a space where any decent, self-respecting woman would usually venture. This career, dead set against women from the outset, was nevertheless the one Rose dared to enter. By the time she became a member of Spoiler's Young Brigade, she was the lone female sharing the stage with Lord Melody, Radio, Lord Caresser and Spoiler. She regarded herself as "The queen of the Young Brigade. Everyone came to see this thin, dry, dry woman flying across the stage."[45] It should be noted, however, that Rose was neither the first nor the only female who successfully made her way onto the calypso stage in Trinidad and Tobago. There are two distinct periods in the history of calypso in Trinidad and Tobago during which women featured prior to Rose's meteoric rise in the second half

TWO

of the twentieth century. From the 1870s to about the end of the nineteenth century, there emerged in Trinidad's Carnival women who were singers, drummers, dancers, stick fighters and so-called prostitutes. Polite society classified them as the "diameter" or "jammettes", whose moral standards of living fell below the line of respectability. Women such as Boadicea, Alice Sugar, Piti Belle Lily, Cariso Jane, Mossie Millie, Ocean Lizzie, Sybil Steele, Ling Mama, Darling Dan, Hard Back Doris, Baje, Annie Coals and Myrtle the Turtle were either the subject of chantwells or chorus back up for Cariso, an early form of calypso.[46] None of these women enjoyed the success that Rose later experienced, but they constituted the background from which her career pivoted.

The first female star of Trinidad's calypso emerged in the early twentieth century. She was Lady Trinidad, whose legal name was Thelma Lewis-Payne, the first woman to sing solo in a calypso tent. She was born in 1914, twenty-six years before Rose. Her musical career began as an entertainer on a cruise ship with a band called The Matchless Boys. Lady Trinidad's debut on a calypso stage occurred in 1935 at the Crystal Palace Tent located on Nelson Street in Port of Spain, and she recorded her first calypso in 1937. Her solo performance was well-received, prompting several encores. A combination of factors would have explained the unusually warm reception that Lady Trinidad received in 1935, despite the prevailing view at the time that a woman's proper place was in the private sphere of the home, not the public sphere of the stage. Supporting her rendition was her husband, who was well respected and accepted in calypso circles.

Additionally, her voice and the composition she performed must have been of superior quality, as evidenced by the several encores she received. Three of the popular renditions of Lady Trinidad are "Nora Nora", "Advice to Young Women" and "Old Man's Darling". Lady Trinidad sang calypso in Trinidad during an era when the few women who dared to perform in the tents were often required to clean the tent before they could even think of singing on the stage.[47] Other female calypsonian pioneers preceding Calypso Rose included Lady Baldwin (Mavis Baldwin), who made her solo calypso debut in 1936 and Lady Iere (Maureen St John), whose husband, Lord Iere was also in the calypso business. Rose's legacy among these early calypsonians, nevertheless, lies in the fact that not only did she join the small but growing number of women in calypso by the 1950s, but she also emerged as the first woman to compete with and triumph over her male counterparts despite the head start that the men enjoyed. By so doing, Rose, unlike her predecessors, paved the way for fuller participation by future generations of women in calypso, such as Denyse Plummer, Singing Sandra and Natasha Wilson.

Calypso Rose has been one of the most prolific calypsonians of Trinidad and Tobago. She attributes this achievement partly to the fact that, unlike many other calypsonians, she composes almost all of the tunes she sings. Winston Devignes, who wrote many calypsos for calypsonians, complimented Rose by observing, "You are the greatest calypso composer of all time; I didn't need to write any for you."[48] Rose has written at least eight hundred calypsos and released approximately twenty albums.[49] Among her albums are *Sexy Short Pants*, *Calypso*

TWO

Queen of the World, *Splish Splash* and *Soca Diva*.[50] Outstanding among this extensive portfolio are classics which have elevated her to the esteemed position of undisputed Queen of Calypso.

At the age of fifteen, Rose released her very first of many calypsos entitled "Glass Thief". At the Croisee in San Juan, Trinidad, Rose witnessed a man steal a pair of spectacles from a woman's face, an incident she found incredulous and which sparked her musical career at the professional level. In this composition, she warned the people of Tobago about the dangers of migrating, temporarily or otherwise, to Trinidad. "Glass Thief" is a social commentary that highlights the difference between crime-prone Trinidad and serene Tobago. When Rose was invited to Tobago in 1956 to sing in honour of Dr Eric Williams, who was visiting the sister isle on one of his meet-the-people political tours of the 1950s, she sang "Glass Thief", one of the only two calypsos she had composed at the time. The other calypso she sang for Dr Williams was "Cancan". It was an important turning point in her life when Dr Williams expressed his approval of her performance and encouraged her to join a calypso tent when she returned to Trinidad.

One of the most outstanding calypsos that Rose has composed and performed is "Fire in Me Wire". The up-tempo, party calypso was first released to the public in the 1966 Carnival season. Its lyrics tell of an old lady whose house caught fire and who called on her neighbour, Ramsingh, for help to extinguish the flames. There can be no missing the sexual innuendo embedded in the lyrics. The old lady's fire alludes to sexual desire for neighbour Ramsingh. The lines of the first verse and chorus read thus:

> I heard a bawling, like somebody crying
> I couldn't imagine what was happening
> I saw this old lady running
> Calling out to she neighbor Ramsingh
> Neighbour, neighbour, O, Lord
> Mey house on fire
> And if yuh hear she
> Fire Fire!
> In mey wire papa
> Ay ya yeye
> O yo yoye
> Fire Fire!
> Ven aca, papito
> Dame mucho agua
> Heat for so[51]

The composition fired the excitement of carnival revellers. It became a strong contender for the Road March title of 1966, rivalling "Obeah Wedding" released by the calypso King of the World, Slinger Francisco, whose calypso sobriquet is The Mighty Sparrow. Rose remembers that the brass musicians, as well as the pan men, were all playing "Fire in Me Wire" at the fetes and other pre-Carnival festivities, and that it was a popular choice for masquerade bands crossing the stage of the Queen's Park Savanah on Carnival Monday and Tuesday. She was certain that she would be crowned Road March Queen in 1966 and was both disappointed and upset when the final result gave the crown to Sparrow's "Obeah Wedding". Not the one to submit without a fight, Rose queried the results. The judges provided two explanations: the first was sexist, while the second was just insipid.[52] They explained that in a musical

TWO

art form almost completely monopolized by men, it would have been against tradition to award the title to a woman. They went on to rationalize their decision by pointing out that "Fire in Me Wire" was a short composition. It only consisted of three verses and a chorus. In time, however, Rose vocalized the hypocrisy, pointing out that the tune had, in fact, become a benchmark for the three-verse calypso, which many of her colleagues soon adopted. The calypso was thus a trendsetter. She was robbed of the Road March title in 1966. Phillip Sander, writing for the airline magazine *Caribbean Beat,* declares that "Rose's Road March breakthrough should have come a decade earlier with "Fire in Me Wire". For years, rumours have it that the 1966 Road March invigilators fudged the figures".[53] As fate would have it, the energy of "Fire in Me Wire" did not die in 1966. The people could not get enough of the tune, and it went on to become a hot favourite in the 1967 Carnival season. To this day, it continues to hold the record of being the only calypso ever to be popular in consecutive Carnival celebrations. Perhaps because of this feat and the lingering controversy it generated, when the government of Trinidad and Tobago declared 2011 the Calypso Rose Carnival Year, she was retroactively recognized and awarded the title of Road March Queen of 1966.[54] The dynamism of this composition is also evidenced by the fact that, no pun intended, it spread like wildfire. It crossed both national and regional boundaries, enjoying international popularity. "Fire in Me Wire" has been translated into nine different world languages, with its last translation being in Japanese.[55] Rose recalls her great surprise and joy when performing in a concert in Morocco: fans were singing the tune along with her in Arabic. Journalist Fayola Fraser, quoting Rose, records,

> In the vibrant port city of Casablanca, Morocco, flung many miles away from home, I stumbled upon a group of French tourists, whose eyes lit up, upon hearing I was from T&T, while knowing almost no English, clapped their hands and sang "fire fire, in meh wire!"[56]

This number is now a calypso anthem.

Calypso Rose completely monopolized Trinidad and Tobago's annual Calypso Queen Competition during the 1970s, a watershed period in her career. No other female in the industry has matched or surpassed her five-year streak (1974–78) of topping the Calypso Queen competition.[57] The most impactful tune in this unbroken string of successes was released in 1975. The title was "Do Them Back". It was shaped by the calypsonian's penchant to encourage women to party heartily. Alas, despite its unquestioned popularity and success in securing the Queen of Calypso crown, for the third time, the Road March title eluded Rose yet again. She was the close runner-up. Patricia Meschino comments that "In 1975 she dropped 'Do Dem Back', ... but again lost the Road March title, supposedly by one point, to Lord Kitchener".[58] He took the 1975 Road March title with the vintage calypso entitled "Tribute to Spree Simon".

Notwithstanding the judges' decision, "Do Them Back" was her first single to reach gold certification in New York.[59] "Do Them Back" selling five hundred thousand copies was undeniable proof that Rose's fan base was growing exponentially. More importantly, it signalled that she was inching dangerously close to supplanting her male competitors.

"Gimme More Tempo" (also known as "Going Down San Fernando" or simply "Tempo") was the 1977 classic that finally earned Calypso Rose the long-awaited Road March title she had pursued season after season. Always confident in the strength of her music, she kept pressing for the prize until she gave the judges a number that was the people's favourite and could not be denied. It was a party tune doubled with a creative and sensible suggestion to Trinidad and Tobago's Carnival Development Committee to decentralize the Carnival celebrations. For most of the twentieth century, Port of Spain, the capital of Trinidad and Tobago, was the centre of the country's Carnival festivities. Rose used "Gimme More Tempo" to widen the festival's geographical spread by extending it from the west to the south. She sang in the chorus:

> Ah going dong San Fernando
> Down dey ha plenty tempo
> Hatters Steel Orchestra jamming sweet
> We go join San Fernandians
> And roll down Coffee St
> So gimme more . . . tempo![60]

Perhaps upset that he did not win the contest in 1977 and hurting more that a woman beat him in a sphere in which, up to this time, men held the pre-eminence, Rose remembers that "Lord Kitchener told me that 'Gimme More Tempo' isn't calypso." She feistily responded, "If that is not calypso, then what is"?[61]

Through "Gimme More Tempo", Rose made history for herself and female calypsonians who came after her. The composition made her the first woman in Trinidad and Tobago to shatter the custom of male singers winning the prestigious award.[62] Keith Anderson reiterates that Rose was the "first woman to break the twenty-year stranglehold that Lord Kitchener and the Mighty Sparrow had on the title".[63] She held this record for twenty-one years until Sanelle Dempster won the Road March singing "De River" in 1991. In addition to Rose and Sanelle Dempster, two other women have taken the Road March crown. Fay Ann Lyons won the competition on three occasions, singing "Display", "Get On" and "Meet Super Blue" in 2003, 2008 and 2009, respectively. The other female calypsonian to take the crown was Patrice Roberts, who teamed up with colleague Machel Montano to win the Road March in 2006, singing "Band of the Year". Calypso Rose's "Gimme More Tempo" was the calypso that shattered the glass ceiling and proved that females in the calypso entertainment industry had what it took to command the streets with their music during the Carnival season and particularly on Carnival Monday and Tuesday.

Calypso Rose produced three unbeatable tunes in the year 1978: "Come Leh We Jam", "Her Majesty" and "I Thank Thee". In an interview with Alvin Daniell, Rose reveals that "Come Leh We Jam" came from a dream she had while in Tortola. In her dream, she saw a tall African lady chanting. She then saw a blackboard with letters on it. She woke and wrote the tune without stopping".[64] "Come Leh We Jam" proved that Rose was a seasoned, experienced and accomplished calypsonian

TWO

whose Road March victory in the previous year was not a fluke. She was clearly in possession of the talent to offer Carnival lovers the music they wanted for their two-day street festival. Her back-to-back successes for the most popular calypso in a Carnival season demonstrated beyond a doubt that Rose was ready for the road.

Whenever she is asked to share her greatest accomplishment in her long calypso career of more than seven decades, Rose never hesitates to reference the titles she won singing "Her Majesty" and "I Thank Thee". "In Her Majesty", Rose alludes to the superior talent of Lord Kitchener and his dominance over the years as Road March champion. The dominant tone of the composition, however, is the fearless optimism with which she challenges her male competitor. Rose sings,

> Everybody hush
> They say it was brainwash
> How that Kitchener is all they does hear
> Them statement is not true
> Plenty people lost they shoe
> It was my new feet
> Make trouble on the street

Oozing with confidence, having dethroned Kitchener once before, Rose optimistically asserts in the chorus,

> They address me
> As Her Majesty
> They say meh music sweet it make for the pan to beat
> It have the skip to jump on Carnival Day
> The brass taking the load

> They call me Queen, Queen, Queen Her Majesty
> Queen of the Road.

Ironically, "Her Majesty", placing second in the Road March competition, was not the tune that made her queen of the road in 1978. Still, it secured for her the weightier title of Top Calypsonian of the year, another accomplishment that made her a female pioneer in the industry. Rose has been careful to point out that "Her Majesty" was one of the few calypsos which she performed but did not compose. She gives the credit for the lyrics of this song to Dennis Stevenson, who composed the words for four Road March and four Calypso Monarch titles. Stevenson was formerly from Barataria, Trinidad, but eventually migrated to Canada. In addition to composing calypsos, he was a playwright and poet.[65] Rose explains that her second calypso monarch-making tune, "I Thank Thee", was crafted with a deliberate and specific objective in mind. She notes,

> I sang, 'I Thank Thee' because I wanted to export my music internationally. So I thanked the musicians, I thanked my mother, the steel pan men, I thanked the calypsonians . . . I thanked everybody, because I knew what I wanted to do. I wanted to export myself and my music. Thank God I wrote that calypso and now my music is all over the world.[66]

For several reasons, this victory was an especially momentous achievement. The Calypso Monarch Competition, more so than the Road March, is the most eagerly anticipated and most illustrious event for the calypsonian. The winner is highly esteemed among peers as the crème de la crème.

TWO

Competitors vie for pride of place as well as attractive monetary and other prizes. Prior to 1978, every winner of the prestigious competition was male. Through "Her Majesty" and "I Thank Thee", Rose secured a mammoth achievement. Not only did she prove that women could hold their own on the calypso stage, but that they also had the talent to triumph over men in an arena men had monopolized for decades. In 1978, Rose was crowned Trinidad and Tobago's Calypso Monarch. She was the first female to hold the distinguished title. Without detracting from Rose's momentous achievement of becoming the first female calypsonian to be crowned Calypso Monarch, it is necessary to identify and correct two myths that have entered the mainstream narrative as a result of this achievement. Rose has often boasted in interviews that she was the first person, male or female, to be crowned as Calypso Monarch. She also claims that the competition title was changed from Calypso King to Calypso Monarch in recognition of her 1978 victory. The records support a slightly different, but significantly different, narrative. The first calypsonian to be crowned Calypso Monarch in Trinidad was not a woman.

Two years before Rose won the crown, the winner in this competition was Chalkdust or Chalkie (Hollis Liverpool). In 1976, Chalkdust's winning compositions were "No Smut for Me and Ah Put on Meh Guns Again".[67] It was the first of nine victories for Chalkdust in the Calypso Monarch Competition. Chalkie won it again in 1977, singing "My Way of Protest" and "Shango Vision". A male calypsonian preceded Rose in winning Trinidad's rebranded premier calypso competition. The record also needs to be set straight about the decision to change the title of this contest. It could not have been, as Rose has repeatedly declared, mainly in recognition of her victory in 1978, since, as we have seen, the name change was already in effect by 1976.

No doubt Rose's runner-up position in the 1975 road march competition and the half a million in record sales of "Do Them Back" must have been decisive factors in the decision to recognize female calypsonians by changing the competition's title from king to monarch. However, alongside Rose's rise in the 1970s was another outstanding female calypsonian whose illustrious career also contributed to changes in the industry. Singing Francine's (Francine Edwards) repeated success as a strong contender in the Calypso King Competition in the 1970s also influenced the Carnival Development Committee of Trinidad and Tobago to consider renaming the title due to changing gender dynamics. In 1972, just one year after launching her calypso career, Francine became the first woman to make it to the finals singing "Carnival Fever" and "Happiness". The results made Francine a new force in calypso to be respected. She placed third behind the two top male calypsonians at the time, Kitchener and Sparrow. It was the first time that a woman came close to rivalling men for top honours in the competition. Francine was again in winner's row, third place, in 1973, singing "Mr Carnival" and "Equal Rights". Two years later, Francine climbed one notch higher, placing second to Kitchener. In her second-place victory of 1975, her renditions consisted of two compositions penned by Winston Devignes entitled "St Peter Say" and "It's a Shame".[68] She had beaten Rose, who in 1975 placed third with "Do Dem

TWO

Back". Indeed, it is to the credit of both Rose and Francine that great strides were made in demonstrating women's ability to hold their own in calypso, despite the biases they faced in the past. It would be wrong to continue to perpetuate the myth that Rose's outstanding achievement in 1978 was solely responsible for the name change of the premier calypso competition in Trinidad and Tobago while overlooking the role of Singing Francine as well as Chalkdust in this evolution of the art form. This proves that Francine's speedy, steady rise in the big competition predated Calypso Rose's ascendancy. Of course, while acknowledging and celebrating Francine's legacy sets the narrative straight, it does not reduce the magnitude of Rose's achievement as the first woman to win the Calypso Road March. Furthermore, while she shares with three other calypsonians, all male, the double honour in one year of winning both the Road March and the Calypso Monarch (Sparrow in 1956 and 1972, Kitchener in 1975 and David Rudder in 1986),[69] she stands alone as the triple crown calypso winner in one year having won the National Calypso Queen Competition, the Road March and the Calypso Monarch all in 1978.

Following her successes as Queen of Calypso, Calypso Road March winner and Calypso Monarch, Rose no longer entered competitions. When questioned about her exit from the Calypso Monarch competition after only one victory, Rose replied that she would not defend her 1978 title because she wanted to make room for younger calypsonians.[70] Yet, she has made a spectacular comeback in her senior years as a calypsonian. One calypso among others, which marks her resurgence, is "Leave Me Alone", featuring soca artiste Machel Montano. It was released in 2016 when Rose was seventy-six years old. It was well received in the 2017 Carnival season of Trinidad and Tobago. More significantly, it became a fight song in different parts of the world, where groups, including the #MeToo Movement, which went viral in October 2017, staged marches in protest against violence against women.[71] The lyrics of this composition reinforced Rose's insistence that women are entitled to enjoyment without sexual harassment and other forms of violation of their persons. She sings,

> Boy doh touch me
> like you goin crazy.
> Let go me hand
> lemme jump up in de band.
> I dont want nobody
> to come and stop me.
> Leave me let me free up,
> myself let me jump up.
> (leave me alone, leave me)
> So leave me alone
> I aint goin home
> So leave me alone
> I aint goin home[72]

Over the course of her long and brilliant career spanning almost seven decades, Rose has released music that has repeatedly placed her above her competitors, male or female, and which continues to enjoy currency among contemporary audiences worldwide.

THREE

Rose has used her calypsos to achieve salient objectives. One of the unmistakable functions of her compositions is to consciously voice gender-related issues and political developments at the national, regional and international levels. In this regard, Rose stands among her colleagues who take the responsibility of the calypsonian seriously as an editorial voice in society.

Rose's exploration of gender relations covers themes such as sexual liberation, workplace exploitation, domestic abuse of women and equality between the sexes. "A Man is a Man", for example, released in 1967, seems on the surface to reinforce the notoriety Rose gained in the formative years of her career for cheapening feminine sexuality. The central argument that Rose constructs in this composition is that a man's value to a woman should consist less in his occupation, race or achievements and more in his ability to satisfy her sexual expectations. The central refrain of the calypso is "you mustn't mind what's his profession … any man can give you satisfaction".[73] The first message that the listener can draw from this number is that

Rose has endorsed the view typically held by male calypsonians that women exist primarily for sexual activity. A more careful inspection of "A Man is a Man", however, reveals Rose's intention of lifting the woman up and out of a needy and subordinate position. The song is infused with a twentieth-century feminist ideology of sexual equality between male and female. It rejects the conservative and traditionalist view that, in selecting a partner, a woman, as the financially dependent party, should prioritize qualities indicating the man's ability to provide for her. Rose throws caution to the wind and becomes a spokesperson for liberation, modernity, female sexual agency and equality with men. She insists that just as in the case of a man, sexual satisfaction and no other criteria should inform a woman's selection of a mate.

Rose's advocacy for female equality with men is reinforced by the popular tune "Do Dem Back" from 1975, which is often mistaken for a party tune. In this calypso, Rose makes bold statements encouraging women to assume social roles traditionally enjoyed by men. The opening line of the calypso chides the female persona who is inhibited and overcome by forlornness because she enters the Carnival fete without her own partner. Rose rebukes her for being in a trance-like state with "your two lip swell".[74] The calypsonian impels the woman to snap out of her coy sullenness and to assert a proactive stand. Unashamedly, Rose declares in verse two, "It have plenty man dey/ Hold on to one and make your play/ Carnival is we fete/ Man easy to get". The calypsonian astutely reminds her female persona that the spirit of gay abandon that characterizes the Carnival celebrations provides the ideal context for the emancipation of women who have been restricted for years by codes of social restraint applied exclusively to their gender. In the last verse, Rose rejects all misgivings and asks rhetorically, "Woman, what you talking at all?" She reiterates, "Remember this is Carnival/ Hold on to any man [and] jam him in the band". The ultimate theme of gender equality is succinctly packaged in the catchy line, "Anything they do you just do dem back".

Another composition that undergirds the point that Rose has promoted a revolution in male/female sexual relationships is the duet she sang with the much younger male calypsonian Machel Montano in 2003, entitled "What She Want". Again, on the surface, the song seems to suggest that the Queen of Calypso is as debased as her male colleagues in demoralizing womanhood. Roy Austin, in a 1976 *Caribbean Quarterly* article, explains the gender system against which Rose is fighting when he notes that, "only the male . . . is expected to engage in sexual exploits. Women who deviate from the mores of the society by being promiscuous are held in low regard".[75] Further analysis, however, reveals Rose's signature and noble demand for a significant shift in the male/female paradigm, giving agency to women. In this song, the woman is not cast in the passive mould that other calypsonians have repeatedly reserved for her. She is not a victim of selfish male lasciviousness; on the contrary, her desires and expectations have become paramount and are the benchmark to which the male is now required to aspire. In the up-tempo dance hall rhythms of this twenty-first-century composition, Rose posits, "Hey young boy tell me what you plan/Big woman don't want no tired man/ Rise up, rise up and make your stand/ Less talk just gih me, gih me action".[76] Calypso Rose does not negate the efficacy of female sexuality, nor does she simply conceptualize it in a degenerate manner. Instead, Rose calls on women to take charge of their sexuality to the extent of crossing traditional thresholds of gender. In an interview on the British Broadcasting Corporation (BBC) Arts and Entertainment Programme, *The Strand*, Rose responded to the critics of her sexual calypsos. She rhetorically reasons, "What is smut? Is sex wrong? If so, why do we have children? Calypso tells the facts of life."[77] Calypso Rose stands as a solid counterpoint to the messages packaged about females by the males who dominate this Caribbean musical genre.

Calypso Rose has given considerable contemplation to the plight of single females in extramarital relationships. She advocates zero tolerance not on the grounds of moral or religious principles but because, according to her logic, it is antithetical to the best interests of women. Renditions such as "Me Doh Want No Married Man", "The Other Woman", "Wah She Go Do" and "Sideman Sweet" record the calypsonian's investigation of this subject. In her 1994 rendition of "Me Doh Want No Married Man", Rose unequivocally calls on women to reject the role of outside mistresses. In the very first line of the composition, she asserts that it is "the worst thing for a single woman to friend with a married man". In her homely, simple yet sensible opinion, she advises that "it is trouble, big, big trouble". She philosophically quips that in this "three-way love section", the outside woman is the disadvantaged "second fiddle". Rose's logical reasoning of the situation is brought to the hilt in the chorus in which she sings, "They tell you dey

THREE

coming/ Whole night you waiting/ Messing up your head/ This time they home with the wife in bed". The chorus underscores the serious psychological frustrations the other woman in the love triangle faces. Rose reinforces her position by pointing out that the unfaithful husband deceives, misuses and abuses the outside woman. He claims that he does not love his wife and that the other woman is the only one for him. Such husbands, Rose observes, enjoy the best of both worlds for "the wife is good to them, and the outside woman treat them like a gem". In the final analysis, Rose adheres to a policy of no compromise in the reverberating line, "Me no want, me no want, me no want no married man".[78] The final resolution of this calypso is a noteworthy example of how a woman's treatment of an old issue in male-female relations can instruct a feminine counterposition.

"The Other Woman", which is part of Rose's 1987 album *Leh We Punta*, reiterates as a warning the disadvantaged experiences of the extra-marital female lover of the cheating husband. The lamentation of the unmarried woman in this emotionally insecure and abusive relationship rings out in the chorus, "I am the other woman/ You don't have no damn compassion/ Anything you want you ring my phone/I have to do your cooking / I have to do your washing /And yuh wife sit down playing queen at home". In other verses of the song, Rose asserts that the outside woman is treated "like a dog just waiting for you to call" and is neglected on birthdays and special holidays. Rose uses the song as a campaign cry to put women on guard against being trapped in such relationships, which she labels unrewarding and demoralizing. She clearly states in the final verse, "I'm sending this message to all women/ Be careful when friending with married men/ You playing second fiddle/Like a thief on handle/ Is heat and burn you getting from married men." Ultimately, the song goes beyond warning and concludes with the compelling advice to "Leave married men alone".

When the tables are turned, however, and the woman is the unfaithful spouse, Rose embraces and justifies the option, comfortable in the conviction that female infidelity is the just response to the failings of the married man. While this is clearly a double standard, it is consistent with the fact, as A. Lynn Bolles explains, that "double standards, sexual inequality and hypocrisy in relations are recounted and acted upon from a woman's perspective" in Rose's calypsos.[79] In the opening lines of "Wah She Go Do," included on the 2009 album *The Best of Calypso Rose*, the artist takes a defensive stance on the woman's behalf. She sings, "I could understand why a woman must have an outside man".[80] She deliberates that unfaithfulness among women is triggered by male infidelity, which renders men physically incapable of satisfying the sexual needs of their legitimate partners, consequently leaving women with no alternative but to find satisfaction beyond the marital bed. In the second verse of the calypso, Rose takes the offensive in offering radical rules of marital engagement. She addresses women thus, "If you have a husband/Give him plenty opposition/ When he start running just laugh/ Don't say anything/ If he pick up a outside woman/ Just show him you can pick up two outside man/ And that's the only way/ A woman should get some respect today".

THREE

Certainly, Calypso Rose's use of the calypso art form makes allowances for female infidelity. Commentators such as Tracy Quan observe that "Wah She Go Do" is typical of Rose's feisty nature and is representative of the bawdy element in many of the calypsos that sing about women.[81] What Quan and others have overlooked, however, is that, in Rose's calypsos, the female perspective on unfaithfulness is given voice for the first time. On the one hand, by exposing the inability of the man to satisfy both his wife and outside lover, Rose shatters the image of the virile male. On the other hand, Rose dignifies the woman by insisting that self-respect is the ideal that fuels her wanderings.

"Sideman Sweet", also part of the album *The Best of Calypso Rose* 2009, is Rose's fullest and most fearless declaration that not only men, as is traditionally the case, but also women, can seek extramarital sexual satisfaction. Without apology, the singer explains in the fourth verse "You men out there listen me and take warning/ Don't believe when you out there cheating/ Your wife ain't horning/ It's like tit for tat and that is a fact/ It's time to pay respect and stop the damn cheating act".[82] As a spokesperson intolerant of unfaithful married men, Calypso Rose declares war, which will continue until men meet the prerequisites for a ceasefire.

The lyrical compositions of Calypso Rose also attack unreasonable men who live at home and cause misery in their women's daily lives. "Don't Touch Me", from the 1984 album *Trouble* and *Solomon*, released in 1986, reveals Rose's scathing criticism of abusive men. The woman in "Don't Touch Me" is a strategist intent on survival despite the unpleasant circumstances of her domestic situation. She is fully cognizant of and exposes the disgusting ways of her common law husband, whom she describes as a "wicked man from Laventille".[83] He is violent, destructive, arrogant, unhygienic, a philanderer and an alcoholic. Despite these flaws in his character, the woman does not leave because she "still love him" and because "good man hard to find". She hardens herself to "Stand meh pain/ I will not complain/ I go hold me strain/ Only for my gain". There is method in her madness. Her survival strategy does not consist only of accommodation to a life of misery but includes, more importantly, stout resistance to either domestic violence or sexual misuse. She warns the man repeatedly in the chorus, "You could do what you like/ You could stay out late at night/ Have yourself a ball I say/ But don't touch me". In a domestic situation where the odds are stacked high against the woman, the coping strategy adopted is definitely positive. It is the resolve of the courageous woman who has both the willpower and stamina to handle her dangerous man.[84]

The woman in "Solomon", first sung in 1984, after sixteen years in a terrible marriage, no longer has the grace to be accommodating. Solomon is guilty of domestic violence to the point of making his wife's face "black and blue".[85] He fails as a provider, and his wife complains, "I cannot see a cent . . . I have to borrow to pay the rent". In his pocket, however, "money-making accident". Additionally, as is the case with many of the male protagonists in Rose's calypsos, he is an adulterer and has even sired children by other women. Although she has suffered for sixteen years in this union, the female persona of "Solomon" has not entirely lost her sense of self and dignity. She musters inner strength and declares, "This time I prefer to be alone". Ready for change, she switches roles from victim to rebel. Without apology, she issues the final ultimatum. She defies Solomon and demands "Get out meh house/ You stinking louse . . . You are a blight . . . Get out let me put some light in my life". Calixte celebrates "Solomon" as a calypso that adopts an aggressive approach to a violent situation, bringing the female protagonist cathartic relief and personal control.[86] It is a decidedly admirable and proactive move on the part of the woman who takes responsibility for recreating a new and independent life for herself out of the pieces that remain after years of spousal abuse. "Solomon" also reinforces one of Rose's signature perspectives on the men who people her calypsos: they are not all as macho as most male calypsonians have presented them.

The most tragic composition in Calypso Rose's exploration of male-female relationships is "Abatina", released in 2016. The calypso draws attention to the ultimate victimization that some women experience in loveless marriages. Abatina, the female persona of the song, is a poor and simple yet honest young woman who marries the charming and wealthy but deceitful and violent Harry, expecting that he will love her. Instead, Harry subjects Tina to continual physical abuse and compels her to be silent. Eventually, Abatina succumbs to Harry's abuse and is buried in the same church where, not long before, her very popular wedding occurred. The rendition offers a stark warning about the deadly consequences of unchecked abuse within marriage. The last stanza of the calypso reads thus:

> Aba Tina oh, who you have there breakin' down the door?
> In the end, Tina was buried

> By the church where she got married
> Aba Tina oh, who you have there breakin' down the door?
> Tina should have outlived us
> Now we pray that she will forgive us
> Aba Tina oh, who you have there breakin' down the door?
> Tina was no deceiver
> Few were inclined to believe her
> Aba Tina oh, who you have there breakin' down the door?

Rose is a feminist calypso activist who consciously shatters the traditional image of the virile male while reclaiming and bestowing self-worth, self-respect, self-empowerment and dignity upon the many women whose daily lives she filters through her timeless renditions.

Rose was very much attuned to the dominant tradition of using the calypso genre to comment not only on social issues but also on the political climate at home, in the region and around the world. This feature of the art form led BBC correspondent Benjamin Ramm to comment that "calypso is among the most political of all musical traditions".[87] The independence movement and the rise of nationalism marked the latter half of the twentieth century in the Caribbean. These political developments provided some fodder for Rose's calypsos.

In the local politics of Trinidad and Tobago, Rose vacillated between support for the People's National Movement (PNM) led by Dr Eric Eustace Williams (first prime minister of Trinidad and Tobago) and the National Alliance for Reconstruction (NAR) led by Arthur Napoleon Raymond Robinson (former Prime Minister and former President of Trinidad and Tobago).[88]

THREE

Rose's loyalty to the PNM took root while she was still quite young. In fact, her coming-of-age experience coincided with the birth of the PNM. Rose shares in a *Caribbean Insight* interview that when she was just a sixteen-year-old, Dr Williams praised her talent, clearly articulating that she was full of potential. The man destined to become the father of the nation, much respected and highly esteemed for taking the country from colonial rule to independence, confidently asserted that Rose had the ability to succeed in the macho world of calypso. Dr Williams's approval was a source of inspiration. Rose recalls her first meeting with the doctor, as he was affectionately called. It was in 1956. The Tobago County Council enlisted her as one of the entertainers invited to serenade Dr Williams on his visit to the island that year. Following her performance of "Glass Thief", the first calypso she composed, Dr Williams shook her hand, complimented her and advised her to join one of the established calypso tents in Trinidad.[89] She followed his advice. In her late teens, not surprisingly, Rose enrolled as a youth member of the PNM and often attended its rallies in and around Port of Spain.[90]

"Respect the Balisier", which Rose released for the 1972 Carnival season, clearly indicates her political support for Dr Eric Williams and his political party, the PNM. In the calypso, she pays tribute to Williams, esteeming him as one of the greatest philosophers of the Western Hemisphere. Rose also uses the calypso to congratulate Williams and the PNM on their victory in the recently concluded 1971 general elections.[91]

By the time Rose released "Turn on the Pressure" in 1973, however, it was clear that her romance with the PNM had crashed on the rocks. It is her most politically charged calypso composition. She had now allied with A. N. R. Robinson and the NAR. In the rendition, she echoes the sentiments common among the Tobago populace at the time that, following the death of Dr Williams, the PNM's policies were becoming increasingly unfavourable to Tobago's inhabitants. She sings,

> Who tell PNM they could stay in power
> Since the doctor dead, the party gone sour
> Turn on the pressure, turn on the pressure, turn on the pressure
> The people tired suffer
> Raise your foot, raise your hand, root them out from the land
> We are Tobagonians
> We've been suffering too long[92]

Rose uses "Turn on the Pressure" to register the economic complaints of Tobagonians that there was inequity in the distribution between Trinidad and Tobago of the revenue generated by oil. Thus, she encourages A. N. R. Robinson to pressure Trinidadians to give Tobago a fair share or face the possibility of segregation.

In 1977, Rose's release of the album entitled "The Action is Tight" reinforced her growing alienation from the PNM. One of the singles on the album, "Have Mercy", consists of a stinging indictment of the poor treatment of Tobago at the hands of PNM politicians in Trinidad. In the calypso, Rose accuses PNM politicians of neglecting Tobago. She attacks the minister of health for what she describes as the hospital's then-terrible state in Tobago. For the dangerous state of affairs involving tourists owning property on the island, she reproaches the minister

THREE

of immigration. Mixing hyperbole with sarcasm, she also laments that the market on Wilson Road is not wide enough to accommodate a donkey and its load. The demands Rose spells out in the calypso include a deep-sea harbour in Scarborough to facilitate the docking of tourist ships, the capital and a radio station to enhance communication between Tobago and the outside world.[93] "Have Mercy" was the first indication that the love affair between Rose and the PNM was not constant. She placed country before politics in her demand for improved conditions in the land of her birth.

"No Madame", released in 1984, addresses a social issue that held significant implications for local politics in Trinidad and Tobago under the PNM regime.[94] Rose uses the calypso to take a stand against employment-related exploitation of female domestic workers. In the chorus, Rose itemizes the slave-like duties that a fictional but representative female domestic in the household of a madam in Princes Town, Trinidad, is required to fulfil. She must "wash the wares/ … clean down meh stairs/ … polish the floor/ … open the door/ … sweep the kitchen/ … empty the dustbin/ … entertain the guest/ … clean up the mess/ … feed the baby/ … bathe the puppy/ … wash the dish/ … wash the saltfish/". In addition to the constant harrying to which the madam subjects the female domestic, there is also the annoyance of being required to show exceptional deference to the employer. The worker complains in dismay 'When I speaking to the madam/ You would not believe me/ I have to be at attention/ Like if I in the army". Furthermore, the maid is dissatisfied with the pay packet. She cries, "I have to wash, starch and iron for the children and the husband/ I working like a elephant for only $20.00 a month". The employee reaches her limit and settles on a subversive plan of action. Rose sings in the third and final verse, "I make up meh mind to leave /And go back in Tobago/ But the madam she start to grieve/ Telling me Rosie don't go/ She turn and she say to me/ She raising my salary/ I say madam don't worry/ I can't take this torment and misery".[95] Even when the tempting offer of an improved compensation package is presented, the domestic stands her ground, making a declaration that a woman's peace of mind cannot be bought. The echo that reverberates throughout the song consists of the two words in the title of the composition, "No Madame", which were sung at the end of each line of the chorus. It constitutes the rebellious chant of a Tobago girl against the endless demands of an exploitative female employer. In an interview, Rose comments on this calypso, making it clear that she consciously took on the role of an activist for women's rights. Rose admits that she is most proud of "No Madame" written at a time when domestics in Trinidad and Tobago were working for a paltry $25 a month. She boasts that "Soon after that song was released, the government voted that no domestic should work for less than $120 a month."[96] Patricia Adkins Chiti testifies that "No Madame" was a call for women's rights and inspired legislation that raised the minimum wage paid to domestic workers in Trinidad and Tobago".[97] Given the lengthy, detailed lists of grievances "No Madame" provides, it is not surprising that its political impact was both direct and effective.

The political calypso through which echoes of Rose's earlier allegiance to Dr Williams and the PNM are heard is her 2009

THREE

release of "The Balance Wheel". The lyrics of the composition can be read as a tribute to the former Father of the Nation and his PNM political party. Rose metaphorically refers to Williams as the balance wheel, an enduring symbol of direction and stability. In the rendition, she admonishes the Trinidad and Tobago citizenry to hold on to Eric and to his successor, George Chambers. She declares that while Williams has departed the physical world, his spirit exerts a lingering, positive force over the nation. Rose uses the calypso to memorialize one of her political heroes and to canvass continued support for a political party with which she was affiliated at times.

The geographical parameters of Rose's political calypsos are not limited to Trinidad and Tobago. In 1979, she turned her attention to the gun violence that marred the Labour Day celebrations, a version of Caribbean Carnival also known as the West Indian Day Parade, staged on the Eastern Parkway in Brooklyn, New York, since 1967.[98] Carlos Lezama, who was born in Venezuela but grew up in Trinidad, led the way in obtaining the licence that permits West Indians in New York to hold the event that promotes and celebrates the culture of Caribbean people in New York.[99] Previously, Harlem was the centre of this Caribbean Carnival in the United States. From the 1920s to the 1940s, it was celebrated in various indoor venues in Harlem and from the 1940s to 1964, revellers took to the streets of Harlem for the festival. Thereafter, New York, the adopted home of Calypso Rose, became the hub for the event. In "Gunplay on D' Parkway", Rose, who, as previously noted, served as an auxiliary police officer in Queens, condemns the West Indians in the diaspora who tote guns in the band and by so doing undermine the festive street party with their violence.

In 2007, in the album entitled *Senior Citizen Day*, she added a composition entitled "Jump Up for Independence", a party tune with strong political tones celebrating the end of British colonial rule in Belize on 21 September 1981. The composition champions democratic rule, describing it as something sweet. Rose congratulates Belize and Belizeans for walking in the right way and wishes the country a happy Independence Day. In the chorus, she jubilantly sings,

> So we go jump up in the road, jump up in the road
> Jump and prance for independence
> We go jump up in the fete
> Jump until we soaking wet
> In the fete for independence.[100]

The high point of Rose's politically sensitive calypso is "Ezekiel Coming", part of her 2000 album *Jesus Is My Rock*. Rose attempts, through this composition, to provide coverage of socio-economic and political events unfolding around the world. It warns about the impending apocalypse overshadowing planet Earth. Rose comments on "Hunger in Somalia" and "Murder in Liberia". She laments the crisis caused by climate change as manifested by "Tornado in Japan", "Earthquake rocking the Caribbean", "Drought in Ethiopia" and "Water flowing over India".[101] "Ezekiel Coming" captures Rose as a keen observer and commentator whose self-imposed duty it is to alert world leaders to the challenges facing their respective countries.

FOUR

In 2010, at the age of seventy, Calypso Rose accomplished a rarity. She released a single "Calypso Queen" that captivated audiences far and wide. In the second line of the ditty, Rose boasted that "my constitution is strong". It was a phrase she had borrowed from calypso veteran Lord Executor, who released a composition in the 1930s titled "They Say I Reign Too Long", defending his rejection of calls to hand over the stage to younger calypsonians.[102] Considering the numerous challenges Calypso Rose has encountered and conquered, including attacks on her claim to Christianity, sexual orientation and health, it is no exaggeration to claim that indeed her constitution is very strong.

The temptation to surmise that Calypso Rose is worldly and non-spiritual is great. After all, since the second half of the twentieth century, she has been a key agent in crafting the calypso, traditionally characterized by a great deal of smutty double entendre. This feature is distinctly antithetical to spirituality. Throughout the sixty-plus years of her career, however, Rose has testified, sung about and exercised her faith in the Christian God.

From birth to the age of nine, while living with her parents in Bethel, Tobago, Rose was indoctrinated in the principles of Christianity. As previously noted, she was the daughter of a Baptist minister. She was "offered up" or christened in the Baptist religion as an infant. In an interview aired on *Caribbean Insight Television*, Rose acknowledged that the Spiritual or Shouter Baptist was the only religion she knew and that she grew up with at least four of its symbols: the calabash, the candle, the bell and the Bible.[103] Her parents, her siblings, and she religiously attended church each Sunday. It was customary for the Sandy family to arrive in the sanctuary at nine in the morning and return home around eight at night.[104] Her father almost strictly adhered to the teachings of the Spiritual Baptist religion and was therefore very upset about Rose's foray into the world of calypso. He unapologetically insisted that members of the Baptist faith served God, but Calypso was the devil's music, and that one cannot serve two masters.[105] Fulani echoes this statement by drawing attention to the "perceived diametrical opposites in Trinidad and Tobago of the 1940s and 1950s. The lewd songs of the calypsonian and the righteous songs of the Spiritual Baptist were thought to serve opposing spiritual allegiances".[106] Rose defied her father not only by refusing to submit to his wishes to quit singing calypso but also by insisting that he was wrong in his damning judgment of the musical genre. From the beginning of her career, Rose theorized that calypso, originating from the word *kaiso*, was integral to her proud African ancestry, about which there was nothing shameful or derogatory. In her mind, far from doing the devil's work, singing calypso was the avenue through which she was

FOUR

fulfilling her God-given mandate to bring joy to the world and to unite people everywhere.

Unlike other calypsonians who seek spiritual salvation in their latter years, such as the Mighty Sparrow and Denyse Plummer, Calypso Rose testifies that her spiritual awakening and personal decision to walk with God began as early as eleven years old. She emphasizes that, as a preteen guided by her own convictions, she was baptized into the Shouter or Spiritual Baptist faith. In an interview with Deborah John in 2003, Rose declared that she never regretted the decision to identify with the Christian church through baptism. "It keeps me sane," she says.[107] It should be noted that at the time of her baptism, Rose was living in Trinidad with her adopted guardians, who, although in a common-law union, were religious. Uncle Aleto Sandy was a member of the Seventh-day Adventist faith, while Aunt Robbie was a Spiritual Baptist. Aunt Robbie, however, was far more lenient than her uncle was and had no qualms about mixing her faith with the festivities of Carnival. Aunt Edith's lifestyle was the model Rose embraced to legitimize the marriage between the perceived worldliness of calypso and the otherworldliness of Christianity. In addition to christening and baptism, Rose participated in the mourning-ground ritual of the Baptists on five separate occasions. She explains that the purpose of mourning is to "cut yourself off from the carnal world to rejuvenate spiritually to seek more wisdom and knowledge".[108] She surmises that each time she mourned, she emerged first as a healer, then as a divider and searcher, and, on the last three occasions, as a mother. In addition to the religious rituals of christening, baptism and mourning, Rose is an ordained elder. Her certificate of ministerial ordination is lodged at the Icons of Tobago Museum. It states that on 17 February 1986, Heavenly Hope House of Prayer Inc. granted Linda McCartha Linda Lewis the credentials of Ordained Minister of the gospel to preach, teach and perform marriage and funeral ceremonies. Thus, she is qualified to be addressed as Mother Rose among Baptist practitioners.[109] Her spiritual grounding is indeed solid.

Rose's fusion of Christianity with calypso was not only rejected by her father but also by various church members in Tobago, particularly women. Christian women from among the Spiritual Baptists, Seventh-day Adventists, Moravians, Catholics and Anglicans associated the lyrics of calypso with vulgarity. Moreover, these sanctimonious women refused to accept that any self-respecting female could maintain her dignity while rubbing shoulders in an entertainment industry monopolized by men.[110] As Nigel Campbell explains, in the 1960s and 1970s, calypso was inherently associated with machismo hyper-sexuality, making it an uneasy bedfellow with the virtues of spirituality.[111] Rose recalls that in the 1950s and 1960s, she was repeatedly summoned to meetings by churchwomen who sought to persuade her to abandon calypso and pursue a more lady-like and Christ-like path. Rose stood her ground. Ironically, she referenced the Bible to justify her resolve, insisting that "I will not be like the five foolish virgins that buried their talent in the soil … [sic] The Lord has given me the ability to write calypso lyrics and create the melody and make the people happy, and I will continue doing that until the day I die."[112] It is not certain whether either Rose or her listeners realized that she was misquoting the Bible. The foolish virgins did not bury their talents. They ran out of oil while waiting for the bridegroom. The burying of the talent is part of the Parable of the Talents recorded in the Bible in the Book of Matthew, chapter 25. The third servant hid his one talent in the ground, and it was eventually taken away from him and given to another, leaving him with none.

Notwithstanding the erroneous biblical quote, Rose nailed her point. She was fully persuaded that singing calypso could not but glorify God. Perhaps for this reason, Deidre Dyer refers to Calypso Rose as the patron saint of women who love to fete.[113] She also defended her position by insisting that while indeed some of the men who dominated the calypso stage were known to indulge in promiscuous behaviour, she herself was above reproach. She drew attention to the fact that far from wearing revealing clothing during her performances, she was always properly clad. Additionally, she boasted that not one of her male colleagues could truthfully claim that she ever indulged in a sexually compromising relationship with any of them. For this reason, they respected her.[114]

In the early years of her career, Rose composed and sang her share of calypsos, which were clearly antithetical to Christian teachings. "The Pudding", which figuratively sings of Caribbean women's shameless worship of the phallus of the black male, and "Palet", which unabashedly acknowledges women's enjoyment of oral sex, are two examples of Rose at her smuttiest. These compositions were released during the 1968 Trinidad and Tobago Carnival. Thus, calypsonian scholar Gordon Rohlehr underscores that "Patterning her performance style on Sparrow . . . she . . . sang on similar themes, acting as counterpart to the male singers, and was in those early days dubbed Queen of Smut by the *Trinidad Guardian* and *Evening News*".[115] In a similar vein Carole Boyce Davies declares that "her stage performance was similar to some male calypsonians . . . including dancing and projecting the microphone as phallus . . . singing songs of men, sex and satisfaction".[116] The church joined in labelling Rose the "Queen of slackness".[117]

In time, Rose made a conscious effort to appease her critics and spiritualize her music. She imported gospel themes into her compositions. Her first attempt to achieve this balance occurred during the Carnival season of 1964, following the devastation wrought by Hurricane Flora in 1963. The hurricane destroyed several properties in Tobago, in addition to which, eighteen people lost their lives. Spirits were low on the island. Rose took the opportunity to comfort the people and to win over her spiritual critics. She muses,

> I wrote a calypso on Hurricane Flora. And what I did, I took hymns and create choruses. I wrote about the devastation, and then in the chorus, I put in hymns such as *Abide with Me*, *Jerusalem My Happy Home*, and *Nearer, My God, to Thee*. And then they started to listen to me. They said that she is singing hymn in the calypso? Something is got to be good there. And then they started easing up on me and started supporting me.[118]

Rose's "Voodoo Lay Loo", released in 1978, is clearly steeped in the musical tradition of the Baptist religion. Voodoo, referenced in the title, is an African religion, as is the Baptist denomination. The central message in the rendition is a desire for a spiritual pilgrimage back to Africa and for reunification with elders, such as the calypsonian's great-grandfather. Rose reinforces the spiritual return to the ancestral land by inserting an African language into the lyrics.

In the latter years of her long musical career, the compositions of Calypso Rose were more steeped in her religious convictions than previously. She released two albums that fused the rhythm of calypso with the spiritual message of Christian gospel. The first of these, released in 2000 by Blue Wave Records, is titled *Jesus Is my Rock*. It consists of eight tracks, including "Call Upon Jesus", "Is Me the Baptist" and "Pray Brother John, Pray". Her second full gospelypso album is called *Just Call Jesus*. She released it in 2003, featuring eleven tracks, including "Pray On", "We Shall Wear a Crown", and "Can Run".[119] Certainly, Calypso Rose repeatedly drew on her spirituality as a muse for her compositions. In her calypso monarch-winning rendition of "I Thank Thee", Rose thanked the Baptist religion for giving her so much wisdom. Calypso critic Gordon Rohlehr has also made the important observation that Rose's prolonged wailing mode of delivery may be an inheritance from her spiritual Baptist/Shouter roots.[120] Ifeona Fulani concludes that "Lewis's spirituality is in many respects the nerve centre of her musical sensibilities; she is forthright about both."[121] Ultimately, Calypso Rose rejected the ultimatum presented to her by her father, the church ladies and the wider society. She was adamant that no one would make her choose between calypso and Christianity. Her strong sense of self has made it possible and plausible to accept herself as a calypsonian attuned to the spirit world.

At the age of seventy-two in 2012, Calypso Rose revealed

that, seventeen years earlier, when she was fifty-four, she had been secretly married to a woman. The ceremony was performed in a Catholic Church in California.[122] Rose has never given birth to her own children but claims her partner's children and five grandchildren as her own.[123] For a long time, Rose remained silent about her homosexual orientation but repeatedly faced snide remarks on the subject. Her colleague and Calypso King of the World, the Mighty Sparrow (Slinger Francisco), often asked without tact, "Why she ain't have no man?"[124] In an interview with Chutney Pride Incorporated, an organization whose mission is to advocate for lesbian, gay, bisexual and transgender (LGBT) people, Rose finally declared boldly, "I am gay . . . I've been married to a woman now for the past seventeen years, 23 September 1994, and I'm not ashamed or afraid to say it right now. That's the reason I'm here tonight to give my sons, my daughters, my brothers, my sisters the support they need in the community."[125] The announcement generated mixed responses. It led some to conclude that her marriage to Aubrey Lewis was a sham and that her claim to Christianity is hypocritical. Some fans were shocked and disappointed. Others accepted Rose's coming out as confirmation of what they had already strongly suspected. And, of course, some esteemed Rose as a respected and influential role model for the LGBTQ community in the Caribbean region, where there is much less tolerance for homosexuality than in the United States and Europe. By this time, Rose was hardly perturbed or deflated by these varying positions. She has refused to accept the view that homosexuality is shameful and sinful. Joshua Surtees reports,

FOUR

> I interviewed Rose at her record label's offices in Pigalle. It was a magical experience. At the end, she got out her guitar and sang a song. Earlier, when I asked her about being a gay icon and about homophobia in the Caribbean, she said, "Why discriminate? Why castigate? God says, 'I make you in my own image and likeness,' so who are you to condemn me? I am a child of God. I did not create myself; I was created by the heavenly master. So why condemn?"[126]

While Rose is no longer ashamed to identify with homosexuality, she has firsthand experience of the tragedy that such an identity can attract. One of her brother's sons, who used to live in New York, was a victim of a homophobic attack. The horrific incident occurred in 2005. Her nephew, Michael Sandy, who identified himself as a gay man, was badly beaten and run over by a vehicle in Brooklyn, New York. He was hospitalized but did not recover from the serious head injuries he sustained. Failing to regain consciousness, one day after his twenty-ninth birthday, he was taken off the respirator that was keeping him alive.[127] Perhaps Michael's murder was one reason why Rose took such a long time before coming out as a lesbian. The fact that she eventually came out, however, is consistent with her reputation as a woman who defiantly confronts and triumphs over the most acrimonious opposition. In the face of condemnation for the sexual lifestyle she has chosen, Rose remains resolute. She refuses to be discouraged by those who judge her on the basis of her sexuality.

Perhaps the greatest battle Rose has fought, and repeatedly won, has been against repeated assaults on her health. She has lived with a speech impediment, survived rape, endured breast and stomach cancer, managed diabetes and heart weakness, suffered severe blood loss, lung failure, arthritis, gout, undergone knee replacement surgery and sustained permanent damage to her left ear due to frequent air travel. As a survivor, she has courageously confronted and repeatedly cheated death. When Rose first migrated from Tobago, the land of her birth, to the sister isle of Trinidad, she suffered from a severe stutter.[128] She was not born with a speech defect. A fall she suffered when she was a child severely affected her ability to speak. Rose narrated the accident in a 2017 interview, hosted by MusicTT's Business of Calypso workshop, in which she was featured. She fell from a high poster bed to the floor headfirst, and it was discovered soon after that the accident impeded her speech.[129] She recalled that when her uncle's common-law wife, Edith Robinson, selected her from among her siblings, she was hardly communicative, fully aware of and embarrassed by the difficulty she experienced when she tried to talk, especially when she was excited. The informal adoption and move to Trinidad, where, at the time, the opportunity for advancement was greater than in Tobago, must have been an overwhelming experience for the young child. Rose recollected that when her aunt enquired about her readiness to embrace the new life in Barataria, Trinidad, she responded merely by sucking her finger and playing with her 'picky' hair.[130] It is, therefore, almost certain that, back in 1949, neither her ten siblings, nor her parents, nor her uncle and aunt in Trinidad could have imagined that this shy girl could take command of her voice on local, regional and international stages to win the admiration of tens of thousands. She herself, on reflection, notes that "*I've come a very long way ... I couldn't speak without stuttering badly back then*". Compounding her speech problem, schoolmates at the San Juan Government School bullied the new girl from Tobago, who often nodded to say yes or no but seldom spoke. Rose quotes their cruel words and actions; "Baw! Talk your dummy, talk, take your finger out your mouth, talk, you can't talk? And every day I went home crying. But I took it".[131] Miraculously, only four years after migrating to Trinidad, Rose transformed from coy stutterer to promising lyricist. What is even more spectacular about Rose's mastery over stammering is that there is no evidence that she sought and benefited from professional help. Rose metamorphosed from being bullied for being an apparent dummy to being a member of the school choir and a regular local feature at weddings, christenings and other community gatherings. By the age of fifteen, she was a new and welcomed addition to Spoiler's Original Young Brigade Calypso Tent[132] without ever sitting through one therapy session with a speech pathologist. In Rose's estimation, it was Edith Robinson, her uncle's common-law wife and her adopted mother, who, with love and patience, nurtured her inherent talent to compose and sing calypso. Tony Hillier concurs that "It was calypso that enabled a thirteen-year-old McArtha Lewis to overcome a debilitating stammer."[133] To this assessment must be added self-determination and discipline, as well as inherent talent waiting to be released, which enabled Rose to beat the odds that threatened to impede her destiny to become one of the greatest composers and performers of calypso music. Today, Calypso Rose boasts that she is stutter-free, "habla mucho" and converses in Spanish and other languages.[134]

At the age of eighteen in her first adopted home, Rose experienced a most traumatically violent yet fairly common experience. She was raped. Accounts of the tragedy record that Rose was returning from a political rally in 1958 held in Barataria by the People's National Movement (PNM).[135] At the time, she was a junior member of the party. Three men subjected her to gang rape. Rose's fighter instincts kicked in. She was no passive victim. Based on the evidence, her predators found it necessary to beat her brutally to perform their most heinous crime. In fighting back, she sustained a broken arm and three fractured ribs. On the surface, these injuries may appear merely as the artist's encounter with victimization. A more profound reading of the events, however, underscores Rose's recalcitrant personality that forbids her from ever giving in to the enemy, however formidable, without a fight. Her reflections on the incident reveal her mettle. While she admits that "you never get over that", on the other hand, she is able to add humour to that painful past by adding "it have sweet sugar down there. I still get calls".[136]

The first major physical ailment Calypso Rose experienced occurred when a medical team diagnosed her with breast cancer in September 1996. At the time, she was fifty-six and was informed that she had just fifteen years to live. In keeping with her indomitable spirit, on the one hand, Rose rejected the prognosis and quipped, "I am sure I am going further than that."[137] On the other hand, however, her dreadful condition brought her vulnerability to the fore of her consciousness. In an interview with Deborah John published on Sunday, 26 January 2003, Rose explained the roller coaster of events and emotions

FOUR

that unfolded following the bad news, which she considered to be a life sentence:

> People need to understand how you feel when you find out you have an illness like that. It was in 1996 when I got the news. I had surgery on October 1, 1996, to remove particles of the breast. Then radiation treatment started from December 14, 1996, into February 1997. After the radiation, I was depressed, so I went to Hawaii to run away from myself. I really went for 10 days, but after three days I realised my family was not with me, and I said what am I doing here and I went back home.[138]

The depression she experienced also manifested in a composition called "I'm Coming Home". Rose sang a few lines of the mournful ditty in the 2017 interview for MusicTT:

> I come here to Mount Zion to go home, Lord
> I come here to Mount Zion to go home
> The angels of God await me home, Lord
> The angels of God await me home
> I could hear the bugle blowing
> And I see the angels coming
> I going home, I going home
> I could see the heavens open
> And the angels, they descending
> I going home, Oh Lord
> I going home[139]

While the mental and emotional confusion Rose experienced as a cancer patient is understandable, it would have been totally uncharacteristic of her not to unlock at some point a positive portal through this dark journey. After her successful breast cancer surgery, Rose, now in a stronger place, confronted medical authorities in New York, lamenting the demoralizing effect of giving cancer patients a limited time to live. She challenged the legality of such a pronouncement and has lived to boast that this course of action is now illegal.[140] Michele Clark, at length, captures and commends Rose's candour, courage, strength, faith and proactivity as a cancer survivor. Dr Clark asserts,

> Calypso Rose's journey through breast cancer illuminates a path of hope and resilience for survivors worldwide. Despite grappling with various health challenges, Rose remained steadfast in sharing her musical talent and advocating for social justice. While detailed information about her personal battle with breast cancer was limited, survivors can glean inspiration from her remarkable strength amidst adversity and her unwavering courage in confronting life's trials. Rose's candidness about her health journey and unshakeable faith highlight the paramount importance of early detection, proactive healthcare, and maintaining a positive mindset. Through her courageous narrative, she empowers others to prioritize their well-being, proactively address medical needs, and discover inner resilience in the face of adversity.[141]

A second bout with cancer, this time in the stomach, reared its ugly head in 1998. It is quite likely that the assurance gained from surviving the first bout of the disease bolstered her spirits. She completed the medical procedure to remove the malignant tumour from her stomach.[142] Nicole Duke-Westfield rejoiced that "Calypso Rose is cancer-free and still full of fire".[143]

Rose's triumphant battles with cancer reinforced her commitment to a healthy diet. Her list of health foods includes

FOUR

ginger, garlic, okra, vegetables, olive oil, water, pumpkin, cat's claws, watercress, banana, dasheen, cassava and other kinds of so-called blue food. As a fisherman's daughter who, up to age nine, lived with him in the seaside village of Bethel in Tobago and accompanied him to the sea each morning, it is no surprise that Rose eats a great deal of seafood, including conch, lobster and a variety of fish. She also relishes sea moss when prepared as a beverage.[144] She declares that she rarely consumes red meat.[145] In addition to paying attention to the nutritional value of the foods she consumes, Rose has also developed over the years habits that have fortified her health. She makes exercise a daily regimen, uses herbal treatments prepared by her brother Lloyd Sandy, is committed to a daily intake of 1000mg of Vitamin C, conducts regular mammogram testing and, strongly believing in the therapeutic value of the sea, takes every opportunity to have a sea bath.[146] Rose also believes that she is fortified by the energy she absorbs from her fans during her performances.[147]

Having proudly taken every course of action to beat cancer, Calypso Rose was ready for another battle, this time of a legal nature arising from her sickness. In 2001, fellow calypsonian Denyse Plummer released a single called "Heroes", a composition by Kurt Alleyne, another colleague in the calypso genre. "Heroes" was one of two calypsos that gave Plummer the calypso monarch crown in 2001. One of the choruses in the rendition declared "Rosie, we sorry . . . No one seems to care right now you suffer/And fighting a battle with breast cancer/ Would we wait till Tantie Rose dead to put honours on her head/ So dread/Always wait till our Heroes dead to put a crown on they head". When the composition was released, Rose was furious.

Contrary to the message carried in "Heroes", she had just received good news in the form of a letter dated 21 February 2001 from the Mount Sinai School of Medicine Radiology Department in New York addressed to McCartha Lewis which read, "We are pleased to tell you that results of your most recent mammogram at Queen's Hospital Center appears to have no suspicious findings."[48] Rose, therefore, concluded that she was cancer-free and considered suing Kurt Alleyne for what she considered "wicked interference". She explained that once "Heroes" hit the airwaves and became popular, she suffered in two irreparable ways; she had to answer questions about her mortality, and promoters were reluctant to book her based on the rumour of poor health. She summed up the dilemma in this way:

> This is not picong, it is serious calypso, and writers have to know that they must check the facts before putting people's names in songs and talking about something that could affect another person in this way. I work for myself. If something is wrong with my health, I stand to lose opportunities, and as a result, my earnings will suffer. In fact, I already have problems explaining to people that I am in good health, since the song became so popular. My old godmother in Tobago, the lady is blind and only hearing the song on the radio. She was crying when she called, saying she didn't know things were so bad and I was suffering so much and asking how long I had to live," Rose said. "Somebody has to pay for that, and the somebody is the writer who said it in the first place. I am fit and as healthy as I've ever been, and I thank God for it.[149]

FOUR

Overcoming breast and stomach cancer was not the end of Rose's health troubles. She has also been diabetic and has been under the surgeon's knife on two occasions for heart surgery. Rose now lives with a pacemaker to help regulate the vital organ but is thankful that she is now off the diabetic medication.[150] In 2009, Rose was critically ill. She lost about four pints of blood, and her lungs collapsed. Looking back on that dark moment, Rose is sure that she died that day, then came back to life. What is remarkable about this near-death experience is the interpretation Rose attaches to it. She opines, "That's how I know the good Lord still wants me here . . . because I have a job to do: bring joy, peace and harmony to my fans and to the world."[151] Out of her multiple experiences with serious illness, Rose shaped an optimistic vision and mission for her life.

Gout was yet another debilitating physical ailment with which the indomitable queen of calypso has battled. The pain that the disease caused her to experience in her feet was so excruciating at times that she just could not walk. In 2007, at seventy-seven years old, Rose checked into a hospital in France to receive treatment for gout. Instead of leaning on hospital staff for emotional support, however, Rose's ebullience came to the fore. She disregarded her discomfort and attracted the workers around her bed as she began to sing the ever-popular "Fire in me Wire" which she first sang in 1966. The warmth and joy she exuded during yet another occasion of physical suffering have, in part, contributed to her healing. With a cherry smile which has become characteristic of her demeanour over the years, Rose went on to release a thirty-second video of herself in which she stated, "Hi! I am back from the hospital. I am doing fine."[52] Rose's courage and exuberance in the face of serious illness have been an inspiration to others and have certainly contributed to her longevity. In 2014, her struggle with gout resurfaced just around the time when regional celebrities, officials, well-wishers and fans in New York gathered in the Bronx to pay tribute to her. Prior to entertaining the audience with a selection of gospelypso and the classic "Fire in me Wire", she testified, "Last week, I couldn't walk. Thank God for bush medicine."[53]

In 2022, in her adopted home in New York, Rose had undergone knee replacement surgery, and towards the latter part of the year, she was at home recuperating. The weak knee must have been responsible for the fall she sustained during her otherwise epic performance at the Coachella Music Festival in 2019.[154] Unfortunately, for a second time, a fellow calypsonian became the source of making her compromised physical condition more stressful than it needed to be. Edwin Ayoung, known in the calypso world as Crazy, visited Rose at her home and secured her permission to post on social media a picture of the convalescent. The image was misconstrued by many who saw it on Facebook. The rumour began to spread that the now eighty-two-year-old queen of calypso was on her deathbed.[155] Rose was greatly perturbed. She complained, "What Crazy did was horrible. I am getting calls from all over the world, Texas, England, France, from people wanting to know what was happening with me." To set the record straight, Rose grasped the opportunity in October 2022 to give an interview to the *Trinidad and Tobago Newsday* newspaper. She insisted,

FOUR

> I am alive and in good health. The only thing that is wrong with me is that I got a new knee. The old one gone and I have to do therapy for the new one because of my weight.[156]

Never the one to accept defeat when life threw her down, Rose proactively attacked the report that she was wasting away on a bed of affliction.

Having successfully fought for her life on numerous occasions, Rose is fully aware of her mortality. In an interview with Deidre Dyer in 2017, Rose shared that the government of Trinidad and Tobago considered offering her money. Her response clearly demonstrated her awareness that life is not guaranteed and that one's legacy is more important than amassing material wealth. She explained,

> They ask me if I want money. I don't want money. I have money. I am seventy-seven. I'll be going home just now . . . I done have a pacemaker. I will not be living long at all, so put my name on a plane and let Calypso be flown all over the world.

Again, in 2022, when the world was emerging from the COVID-19 pandemic, she released a statement explaining,

> My dear friends, it is with great sadness that I have to cancel my tour dates this summer. The virus and my health situation will not allow me to come to France. But I'll be back next Spring with new songs, and I hope you will love them.[157]

The illnesses Rose has experienced over the years have been chronically life-threatening. She has lived, however, to celebrate her eighty-fifth year in 2025 and has proven that she possesses the mettle that makes for a strong constitution.

FIVE

The life and music of Calypso Rose have so fired the imagination of her fans around the world that several films and productions featuring the Caribbean artiste have been produced. The first of these was *Bacchanal Time* released in 1978. It is one of the first entirely locally produced films in Trinidad and Tobago. The locations, music, technical equipment, crew, actors and actresses were all locally based.[158] Trinidadian Kamalo Deen wrote, directed and edited the film. It is a presentation by Pempaleh International Productions Limited, with Wahid Omardeen as its producer. *Bacchanal Time* is part of the Carnival celebrations in Trinidad and Tobago, and the central activity is an island-wide stick-fighting competition held at Skinner Park in San Fernando on Carnival Sunday night. It culminates with the early-morning J'ouvert jump-up, beginning at 4:00 a.m. on Carnival Monday. The actions leading up to the climax consist of a comedy of errors that appropriately captures its bacchanal elements while remaining true to the rich and diverse cultural realities of the Indian and African characters who people the film.

FIVE

The film's pulsating rhythms are largely filtered through the calypso music of Rose and other calypsonians such as Shadow, Trinidad Rio and The Mighty Wanderer. The presence of Rose in the film is first captured through one of her calypsos played in the background. This number is entitled "Burn Dem". As the plot unfolds, Rose's role thickens. She is well known to the two main female characters, Elsa and Shanti, who are the spouses of the two champion stick fighters in the film, Bondon and Gopie, respectively. The women seek out Rose at the Seaman and Waterfront Workers Trade Union (SWWTU) Carnival tent, where the artist is on stage singing "Fire in the Area". Rose becomes critically involved in the action of *Bacchanal Time*. Elsa and Shanti meet her backstage and ask for her assistance in getting to Skinner Park in San Fernando, where their husbands are scheduled to battle Tiger, another stick-fighter. Rose agrees, speeds to the centre of the action in her car with her two friends and ultimately enables them to witness their husbands' victory in the gayelle, or fighting ring. *Bacchanal Time* both captures the popularity of Rose as a calypsonian by the 1970s and contributes to her popularity. The director of the film reveals that it was shown for four consecutive weeks at the Deluxe Cinema in Port of Spain, six weeks at the Empire Cinema in San Fernando, moved to New York, opened on Broadway, and was also a hit in Brooklyn, Boston and Toronto. The government of Trinidad and Tobago also booked and paid for the film to be shown to schoolchildren in the twin republic.[159] *Bacchanal Time* reinforces Rose's stardom in the calypso world.

Calypso Rose collaborated with fellow calypsonian Lord

Kitchener, also known as Kitchie and the Grand Master, to produce a calypso documentary entitled *One Hand Don't Clap*. Kavery Dutta Kaul, originally from Bengal, India, directed and edited the production.[160] It was completed in 1988 and first released on 28 August 1991 by River Films. The director informed Trinidad and Tobago Television in a 2022 interview commemorating the centennial of Kitchener's birth that the documentary reached wide audiences in the United States, Europe, Africa and Asia. The documentary reflectively captures the careers of the two calypsonians it features, the competitive relationship between them and their roles and responsibilities as senior practitioners of the art form to a new and younger generation of calypsonians who are moving away from traditional calypso to the modern variation called soca, a fusion of calypso and soul music. In the documentary, Kitchener expresses the view that it is soca, rather than the traditional, slower calypso beat, that will propel the local music of Trinidad and Tobago onto the international stage. At the time the documentary is produced, Lord Kitchener is just some months shy of his seventieth birthday. He provides an overview of his role as cultural ambassador in the 1940s when he transported calypso to London and, by extension, to the wider public in the United Kingdom. Lord Kitchener shares recollections of his early years in calypso with other old-timers of the trade, such as Lord Pretender and the Growling Tiger. When questioned about his most successful album, he confidently responds that "Sugar Bum Bum" has sold better than the rest.[161] The documentary also highlights Kitchener's 1987 classic "Pan in A Minor". When the spotlight turns to Rose's introspections, she remembers her journey to becoming the greatest female calypsonian of her time, as evidenced by multiple consecutive victories in the National Calypso Queen Competition, as well as being the first woman to win the Road March title and to be crowned Calypso Monarch. One of her many compositions featured in the film is *Solomon*. Both she and Lord Kitchener converse about their fierce competition in the 1960s and 1970s to put on the road the most popular tune of the Carnival season. It is from this section of the documentary that the production's title emerges. Rose and Kitchener concur that in battling each other, they were sharpening each other's talent. In one scene of the documentary, Rose even credits Kitchener for giving sound advice to enhance her performance. This is a recognition of their interdependence, which is the meaning of the folk saying "one hand don't clap". As each scene of the documentary unfolds interspersed with narration, rehearsals and on-stage performances by Rose and Kitchener, snippets from Carnival festivities such as masqueraders in the streets and steelpan men with the instruments around the neck, the film gives way to a younger generation of calypsonians such as Black Stalin, the Mighty Duke, David Rudder and Natasha Wilson singing the more up-tempo version of soca at Kitchener's Calypso Revue. *One Hand Don't Clap*, therefore, presents a trajectory extending back to the past as embodied largely by Lord Pretender, the Growling Tiger, Kitchener and Rose. It extends to the present, epitomized by David Rudder and Black Stalin. It ultimately points to the future embodied in the young Natasha Wilson. Interestingly, the relationship between the two major characters is not limited to rivalry but is expanded to underscore their important roles as adjudicators and Masters of Ceremony for the younger performers. The past and present, rivalry and interdependence, the old and the young, and traditional calypso and soca are brought together in this brilliant documentary, featuring, in part, the musical career of Calypso Rose.

With the objective of recapturing calypso music at its original and classical best, in 2005 Pascale Obolo edited and directed *Calypso at Dirty Jim's*, selecting as his cast the last of the great calypsonians, including the Mighty Sparrow, Bomber, Lord Superior, Relator, Mighty Terror and, of course, Calypso Rose.[162] The gathering of these senior, seasoned and successful calypsonians was filmed at Dirty Jim's Swizzle, a thriving entertainment centre opened in the late 1950s and located in Port of Spain, the capital of Trinidad. It exists no longer. On the site where the edifice was erected, a car park owned by *The Express Newspaper* stands. In the calypso documentary, Rose and her colleagues join their voices to perform "Rum and Coca-Cola", a signature calypso in the history of the musical genre. Rupert Westmore Grant, a Trinidadian calypsonian whose sobriquet was Lord Invader, is credited with composing the lyrics in 1943, while another Trinidadian permitted him to use the melody. Soon thereafter, Morey Amsterdam, claiming that he had written the song for the Andrews Sisters of New York, through whose rendition this calypso, in particular, and calypso music in general, became internationally popular, was forced to pay royalties to Lord Invader while retaining its copyright. The star-studded cast of *Calypso at Dirty Jim's* also came together to sing Sparrow's well-known composition about

FIVE

American servicemen in Chaguaramas, Trinidad, during World War II entitled "Jean and Dinah" and the calypso choir in the film also sang "Shame and Scandal in the Family" made famous by its multiple covers, including versions by Fitzroy Alexander also known as Lord Melody, Sir Lancelot, Blue Blasters and the Wailers. There are also the French Guadeloupian and Portuguese translations of "Shame and Scandal in the Family". The emphasis that this musical documentary places on the originality of the Trinidad calypso and the best among its many practitioners is captured in the space allocated to extempo. Calypsonian Relator explains:

> At Dirty Jim Bomber came here and sing a verse
> In extempo you're not allowed to rehearse
> You have to show how much blasted talent you got
> By singing your lines right here on the spot[163]

Unlike the other productions in which Rose is the central figure or co-star, the male calypsonians, not surprisingly, given that the film looks back to the good old days of calypso, dominate the scenes. Ironically, it is this gender imbalance in the cast that enables Rose to shine among the celebrity band of musicians at *Calypso at Dirty Jim's*.

The award-winning calypso documentary *Calypso Dreams*, released in 2004, gathers a wide array of calypsonians, including Calypso Rose. The film's main objective is to trace the roots of the musical genre. It also seeks to define the art form, pays tribute to older calypsonians such as the Grand Master Lord Kitchener, celebrates Trinidad as the motherland of all Carnivals, examines the history of women in calypso and clarifies the contribution of American-based Harry Belafonte to the development of calypso. It does so by interspersing calypso renditions with narratives by calypsonians while capturing local scenes in Trinidad. In an early monologue of the documentary, Calypsonian Brigo comments that "Calypso is the poor man's newspaper. A calypsonian is the people's spokesman." When the camera first focuses on Rose, she reiterates that, despite being a woman in a male-dominated industry, she is unstoppable. She declares, "I am like a river overflowing its banks. You try to stop me, I am going to find room to pass."[64] This is exactly what Rose does in *Calypso Dreams*. The documentary's scenes are filled with the faces and voices of male calypsonians, but every so often, the unmistakable presence of Rose is caught on camera. In the section devoted to interrogating the history of women in calypso, Rose, along with two other female calypsonians, Denyse Plummer and Singing Sandra, speaks out. Singing Sandra highlights the difficult experiences, especially in the 1960s and 1970s, of women singing calypso alongside men. Outstanding among these female voices is Calypso Rose's. She clarifies the often-mistaken concept that she is the first woman to sing calypso in Trinidad and Tobago. Rose underscores that Lady Iere was one of her forerunners. Sitting in white shorts and a white T-shirt between male calypsonians, Double D and Crazy, with three others in the background, Rose also performs "Fire in Me Wire", the signature piece among her many compositions. After this performance, she reminds listeners that she was denied the road march title of 1966 because she was putting "licks" on the men who were too embarrassed

FIVE

to allow a woman to upstage them. Rose has two other key appearances in the documentary. She is the accompanying guitarist for Lord Funny, showcasing her talents as both a vocalist and an instrumentalist. Finally, she sings a verse and chorus of one of her songs advocating the right of women to be sexually liberated, "A Woman Must Have an Outside Man". Geoffrey Dunn and Michael Horne directed *Calypso Dreams*, while Dunn, Horne, Mark Schwartz and Eric Thiermann served as producers. *Calypso Dreams* won the Best Caribbean Documentary award at the Jamaican Film Festival in 2004 and was the audience favourite at the DC Film Festival, the Pan African Film Festival and the Mill Valley Film Festival in 2004.[165]

In 2009, the eighty-minute documentary entitled *La Diva Rose* was released. Philippe Djivas and Jean-Michel Gibert produced the film, while the Cameroon-born filmmaker living in Paris directed it.[166] A central theme of the production is Rose's successful challenge of her male competitors. It first reveals the difficulties she endured in the early phase of her career, then ends on a triumphant note, saluting her resilience. Geographically, the documentary covers important milestones in Rose's life and career. It begins in Tobago, where she was born, transitions to Trinidad, where her career took flight, stops off in New York, the current home of the artist, crosses over to Liberia, for whom Rose served as a UNICEF Goodwill Ambassador, and ends in Paris, where Rose has experienced a resurgence in her latter years. *La Diva Rosa* captures almost every important stage in Rose's life, work and accomplishments. When it was released, it was submitted to the 2009 Hot Docs

Documentary Festival in Toronto, Canada, and received rave reviews from the audience.[167]

Another film featuring calypsonians from Trinidad and Tobago and starring Calypso Rose is *Calypso Rose: Lioness of the Jungle*, completed in 2011 and released in the United States in April 2012. The title hammers home the point that Rose had to be a fierce female animal, none other than the queen of the jungle, to endure and triumph over the opposition she faced both from the church and male calypsonians in choosing to make calypso her career. The Mighty Sparrow, the Mighty Shadow and Gypsy, along with others, appear from time to time in the documentary to sing the praises of the diva of calypso. Ultimately, however, the film gives centre stage to Rose herself. Her music, her personal life, her musical achievements, her tragedies and her vision fill every scene of the production. It opens with one of her many compositions, "Israel by Bus", which symbolically refers to the people of the Caribbean as the chosen people of God, heading for the promised land. The documentary's narration, interspersed with footage, recalls that Rose joined the calypso fraternity in 1955 and that it is still going strong almost six decades later. In her own words, "The stage is my life."[168] The diva reflectively rejoices in the fact that she won the Calypso Queen competition five years in a row and has under her belt four national calypso titles. She therefore sees herself as the woman in an industry once dominated by men who broke gender barriers and paved the way for the younger generation of female calypsonians. One of the tragedies Rose shares in *Lioness of the Jungle* is her encounter with rape and the impact of that trauma on her relations with

FIVE

the opposite sex. From the land of her birth, the film revisits some of Rose's life's journey destinations, including Paris, New York and Africa, underscoring that Rose exported her music worldwide. For Rose, ending in Africa holds personal, cultural, motivational and spiritual significance. She reveals that Africa has always exerted a strong pull on her consciousness.

The motherland has been one of her most significant muses. It provided her with visions, some of which she turned into compositions such as "Come Leh We Jam". The journey to Africa, Benin in particular, fulfilled Rose's lifelong desire to physically connect and identify with the continent of her ancestors. She boasts in the film that her maternal great-grandmother, Martha Paul, who was originally from Guinea, was stolen from the land of her birth and brought to work in the Caribbean as an enslaved person. Pascale Obolo, a French Cameroonian filmmaker, worked with Rose for four years to direct *Lioness of the Jungle*. Maturity Production, Trinidad and Tobago Film Company and Dynamo Productions produced the film, celebrating Calypso Rose as an exemplary ambassador of Caribbean music and culture. PBS, France TV and Trace TV have all aired the documentary.[169]

To date, the final production featuring Rose is the musical entitled *Queen of the Road: The Calypso Rose Musical*, written and directed by Rhoma Spencer. Roger Gibbs superintended the musical elements while Rawle Gibbons headed dramaturgy. It was first viewed at the Central Bank Auditorium in Trinidad in May 2024. The jukebox musical moves backwards, beginning with one of Rose's latest accolades: the 2017 award in Paris, the Victoire de la Musique. The series of flashbacks covers

Rose's thank-you speech, embodied in her calypso-winning number of 1978, entitled "I Thank Thee", invocations of her great-grandmother, her early life in Trinidad and Tobago, as well as the many triumphs and weaknesses that defined her life and musical career.[170] The musical is divided into four acts covering approximately forty of her calypsos. It is patterned after Trinidad and Tobago's Prime Minister's Best Village Trophy Competition, which allows for a smooth flow from vocal performance into dance, drama and a costume parade, all of which capture Rose's fearless journey as a woman into a sphere dominated by men.[171] Two actresses play Rose: Thara Howe portrays Rose as a child, while Stacey Sobers embodies both the young adult and the older Rose. The musical is a celebration of a daughter of the soil who overcame many obstacles to win the heart of her people and the world through her music.

While Rose is unquestionably a star in her own right, throughout her career, she has collaborated at various levels with several celebrities from the national, regional and global entertainment industry. As early as 1967, Rose appeared on stage with the late great reggae legend, Bob Marley. The first shared performance took place in the Grand Ballroom in New York City. Rose returned with Bob Marley to the Grand Concourse in the Bronx in New York on New Year's Eve 1969. She recalls that, partly because of Harry Belafonte's hit "Banana Boat Song", which popularized calypso music in particular and Caribbean music in general in the United States, the crowd went wild when she and Bob Marley took the stage. On a subsequent occasion, the two were guest artists in a festival in Orlando, Florida. Rose also reveals that she toured

FIVE

with Marley in London. She declares that Bob Marley, while respected as the king of reggae, loved calypso and enjoyed dancing to the songs composed by the Queen of Calypso.[172] She describes him as a spiritual man, noting, "He never lifted his guitar off the stage without putting his head onto the wall and praying."[173] Rose testifies that there was mutual respect for each other's talent and that she learnt a great deal about music and show business from Bob Marley, although she distanced herself from his use of marijuana. Rose greatly admired Bob Marley and admits that "Bob is the vocalist I love listening to the most."[174] Ras Kefim comments that the Rose/Marley tours brought together the folk music of Trinidad and Jamaica, both of which, by the end of the twentieth century, focused primarily on protest against injustice. Kefim aptly concludes that the interaction between Rose and Marley was on equal footing between two giants of Caribbean music.[175]

Another outstanding internationally known and celebrated musical superstar with whom Rose collaborated was the former indisputable King of American pop, Michael Jackson. In 1978, Michael Jackson and his four brothers who formed the Jackson Five were on tour in Trinidad and Tobago. They held two concerts sponsored by the company called Spektakcula Promotions directed by Frank and Claude Martineau. One of the concerts was held at the Queen's Park Savannah, located in the capital city of Port of Spain, and the other in the southern city of San Fernando. Rose, who had just been crowned the first-ever female Calypso Monarch of Trinidad and Tobago, was one of the local artistes invited to share the stage with Michael Jackson and his brothers.[176]

By the end of the twentieth century, Rose had performed alongside the legendary South African musical icon Miriam Makeba. She also rubbed shoulders with the so-called King of Timbales, the American-born Ernest Anthony Puente, popularly known as Tito Puente, musical master of mambo and Latin jazz. She had concert appearances with Mahalia Jackson, the esteemed American Queen of Gospel music and with the five-time Grammy Award-winning American singer Roberta Flack, who, in some of her renditions, combined gospel, soul, flamenco and jazz.[177]

In recent times, Rose has worked closely with contemporary musical artists to produce a number of releases that have diversified her musical range. Rose's very successful *Far from Home* album, released in 2016, features a tight collaboration with rock star Manu Chao, born in France but based in Barcelona. He is multilingual. Chao remixed three of the calypsos on the album: "Far from Home", "Leave Me Alone" and "Human Race". Chao's vocals are repeatedly spotlighted in these three renditions. In "Leave Me Alone", in particular, the voice of fellow countryman, superstar soca artiste Machel Montano, stands out.[178] Rose embraced Machel Montano again in 2019 for her duo rendition of "Young Boy".[179] Additionally, in 2019, on the album *Calypso Rose and Friends*, she brought fellow female Trinidadian Nailah Blackman into her circle to sing with her on a piece called "Baila Mami". The lyrics are both in English and Spanish. Rose's 2022 cover of the calypso "Watina", originally the title of an album released in 2007 by Andy Palacio, one year before he died, consisted primarily of collaborations with musical giants of Belizean origin.

FIVE

Grammy Award-winning guitarist Carlos Santana was the key instrumentalist in the re-composition. Musical accompaniment was also provided by the band Garifuna Collective, which Palacio co-founded.[180] The producer of this calypso, Ivan Duran, is also from Belize. The cover was a tribute to Palacio's memory and legacy, as well as an affirmation of the Garifuna people, whose culture is, in recent times, threatened by forces that could lead to its erasure. "Watina" reinforces Rose's close association with and support of Belizean culture spanning more than four decades. "Watina" is part of Rose's 2022 album, *Forever*, produced by the Belizean Ivan Duran. It is a compilation of fourteen timeless calypsos sung in collaboration with Machel Montano, Jamaican dancehall icon Mr Vegas, Toulouse rapper Oli and electro duo Synapson.[181] Rose's collaboration with young musicians, both male and female, from home and abroad, representing different musical genres, is significant. It shows that indeed she no longer views the stage as a competition. These musicians are her colleagues. It confirms her comfortable acceptance of not only calypso but also soca, jazz, pop, the blues and the harmonious blends they can create when artistically combined. It also closes the gap between older and younger generations of musicians worldwide.

SIX

Apart from the many titles Rose won for her supremacy in calypso competitions, the artiste has been frequently honoured both at home and abroad in recognition of her great contributions to the development and promotion of culture and for her activism, especially in advocating for the rights of women. In this regard, she is the most decorated calypsonian in the world.[182] Rose is not only a recipient of a multiplicity of awards but also a magnanimous benefactor who focuses particularly on underprivileged children and health institutions.

From the home government of Trinidad and Tobago, Rose is the recipient of three national awards.[183] The first was the Public Service Medal of Merit (Silver), awarded in 1975 in recognition of her mastery of and contribution to the culture of Trinidad and Tobago. In 1975, Trinidad and Tobago was one year shy of becoming a republic. Thus, it was by the order of Her Royal Majesty, Queen Elizabeth II of England, that Rose received this first national award. In the year 2000, after a career of singing calypso at home, across the Caribbean

SIX

region and internationally for forty-five years, the government of Trinidad and Tobago deemed it appropriate to bestow on Calypso Rose yet another national award. The second was higher than the first. It was the Humming Bird Medal Gold. The full ascription governing the Humming Bird Medal Gold of Trinidad and Tobago is an award given for loyal and devoted service beneficial to the state in any field, or acts of gallantry. Calypso Rose received the national gold medal for her contribution to culture. Following the resurgence of her career by the turn of the new millennium, in 2017, the decision was taken that Rose was worthy of the highest national award of Trinidad and Tobago. The Order of the Republic of Trinidad and Tobago was bestowed on McCartha Linda Sandy-Lewis on 24 September 2017. She was the first calypsonian to receive this honour and, thus far, only one other calypsonian, Chalkdust (Hollis Liverpool), has been similarly recognized.[184] In 2017, the local government also granted Rose a diplomatic passport in recognition of her winning the French Victoires de la Musique.[185] Additionally, on the island of her birth, Rose was inducted into the Tobago Walk of Fame in 1993 as a charter member and, in 1999, the Tobago House of Assembly named its new hospital the McCartha Lewis Memorial Hospital. The tremendous pride with which fellow Tobagonians embrace Rose was clearly demonstrated when, in 2015, the Division of Community Development and Culture of Tobago presented her with a wooden bust of herself. In the following year, the then chief secretary of the Tobago House of Assembly, Orville London, announced the launch of the Calypso Rose Award to "ensure that people remember your contribution".[186] To capture greater public visibility in the land of her birth, in October 2025, the Tobago House of Assembly unveiled the name of a new street sign in Scarborough. The road formerly known as Milford Road was rechristened Calypso Rose Boulevard.[187] Rose counted the gesture as a signal honour. The multiple recognitions of Calypso Rose by the government of Trinidad and Tobago reveal that, incrementally, the people and leaders of her country came to appreciate the genius of her musical offerings and her role in exporting the music and culture of Trinidad and Tobago around the world.

Another local entity that paid tribute to the greatness of Calypso Rose's talents by heaping honours upon her was The National Action Committee for Women in Trinidad and Tobago. In 1991, this body presented Rose with the Most Outstanding Woman in Trinidad and Tobago of the Year Award, as well as the Most Outstanding Female in the Field of Music in Trinidad and Tobago. In 2012, the regional air carrier, Caribbean Airlines (CAL), concurred that the best way it could esteem the genius of the female calypsonian was by naming one of its Boeing 737 aircraft after Calypso Rose.[188] Two years later, at its annual graduation ceremonies, The University of the West Indies, St Augustine Campus, conferred on Calypso Rose an Honorary Doctor of Letters. The premier academic institution of the Caribbean paid tribute to Rose as a calypsonian and cultural ambassador.[189]

In the wider Caribbean region, Belize has stood out amongst its neighbours for its appreciation and honour of Calypso Rose. In 1982, in recognition of her contributions to raising awareness of Belizean culture regionally and internationally, the people

SIX

and government of Belize made Rose an honorary citizen, a distinction she richly deserved, as previously demonstrated. Recognition from Belize did not end with the conferring of honorary citizenship. On the occasion of the twenty-fifth anniversary of independence in Belize in 1987, Rose became the recipient of the National Belize Music Award. The gesture was a clear indication of the extent to which the country embraced Rose as one of their own. Again, in 1988, Rose received a Commendation for the Development of Arts and Culture in Belize from the National Arts Council of Belize. Long after she received awards from Belize in the 1980s, Rose continued to use her music to promote the country's culture.

Another Caribbean country that heaped honours on Calypso Rose was Jamaica. Although Rose has not resided in Jamaica for any considerable period, the government of Jamaica offered her honorary residency in recognition of and appreciation for her contribution to raising awareness on the cultural front.[190]

The African nation of Liberia has also honoured Calypso Rose for her efforts to use her music to promote its culture and for her activism in raising international awareness of its struggles with developmental issues. In 1986, Rose became ambassador-at-large or honorary ambassador of Liberia, complete with a diplomatic passport.[191] The title was given in conjunction with the Recognition for Achievement in Human Progress from the Concerned Citizens of Liberia Organization. Rose explained in an interview with Anu Lakhan that as an ambassador for Liberia, she represents the country in the United States.[192] An elementary school in Liberia is also named in her honour.[193] Liberia's decision to honour Calypso

Rose was influenced largely by her calypso entitled "Pepper Soup". The composition popularizes one of Liberia's most well-known culinary dishes, prepared with a variety of seafood and seasoned with copious amounts of pepper. At times, it is eaten with fufu. The dish is served at almost every party and other social gatherings in Liberia. In the chorus, Rose warns, "Once you drink that pepper soup, you can't get away/ in Liberia, you have to stay."[194] By choosing Liberian pepper soup as the theme of one of her calypsos, the musical ambassador has put Liberia on the international culinary map. A second major award offered to Calypso Rose from the African continent was the African Festival Achievement Award, which she received in 2011.[195]

Rose's reputation as one of the most recognized musicians in the world also rests on her having received multiple prestigious awards from the French. She is the first and only calypsonian to date to win a French Grammy. In 2017, Rose's *Far from Home* album, released in 2016, won the top prize for Best Album in the World category at the 32nd annual French music award ceremony known as Les Victoires de la Musique, the French equivalent of the Grammy Awards.[196] *Far from Home* ousted the albums *Music of France* by the rock group known as Acid Arab and *Born So* by Rokia Traore to win the French Grammy.[197] It went platinum in France soon after its release. Not even the music of the Mighty Sparrow, Calypso King of the World, has penetrated the international scene to such an extent. This achievement attests to the timeless greatness of Rose's calypsos. In the following year, 2018, the French heaped yet another accolade on Calypso Rose. This time, the French Society of

SIX

Authors, Composers and Publishers (SACEM) presented her with the Grand Prize of the World Music Grand Prix.[198] Rose is certainly a prolific composer with hundreds of compositions in her name. It is no wonder that she clinched this prize. France recognized and esteemed Calypso Rose for the third time in 2020, naming her an Officer of the French Order of Arts and Letters, the highest French award in the Arts and Culture category.[199]

The honour of being offered the key to the city has been bestowed on Calypso Rose on multiple occasions. In her own Trinidad and Tobago, the mayors of two cities, Arima and Port of Spain, offered her the keys to their cities in 2003.[200] Newspaper writer Wayne Bowman covered the story when Mayor Murchinson Brown of the city of Port of Spain presented Rose with the keys. It began with a motorcade including a music truck which left the Arima Dial at 10:00 a.m. The next stop was City Hall, located on Knox Street in Port of Spain. By 6:00 p.m., the motorcade had made its way to Club Caribbean on Wrightson Road. One of the highlights of the event was the launch of a remix of Rose's *Fire in Me Wire*. Soca artistes invited to serenade Rose at Club Caribbean included KMC, Bunji Garlin, Machel Montano, Iwer George and Crazy.[201] A third mayor in Trinidad, the Mayor of San Fernando, presented Dr McCartha Linda Sandy Lewis with the key to the city in 2017.[202] It was no coincidence that the ceremonial act honouring an international icon took place on the eve of International Women's Day.

As an international traveller and ambassador of the music of Trinidad and Tobago and the wider Caribbean who has staged numerous performances with an enormous global fan base, Rose has also been given the keys to cities outside of the land of her birth. In fact, Trinidad and Tobago was not the first to take this initiative. In 1993, Rose received the keys to the city of Ontario, Canada, from the Mayor of St Catherine, Joseph Reid.[203] On reflecting on this recognition, Rose declares,

> I figured he was aware of my music that included a calypso I composed about Quebec Frenchmen loving to 'wine'. It was quite an honour to be recognized with the key to a Canadian city. At the time, it was the biggest recognition that I had received.[204]

Rose also holds the keys to Lauderdale Lakes, Florida.[205]

The music and activism of Calypso Rose have also captured the attention and respect of transnational bodies. Ginelle Greene-Dewasmes comments on Rose's appointment as United Nations International Children's Emergency Fund (UNICEF) Ambassador for former child soldiers by noting that:

> Calypso Rose's career spans decades marked by her ability to infuse her music with social and political commentary. Her lyrics often address issues of gender equality, social justice, and Caribbean identity, resonating with the struggles and triumphs of the diaspora. Her music also addresses other resonating global topics such as domestic violence, sexism and racism.[206]

Rose's UNICEF appointment was no mean feat. These ambassadors are among the most recognizable faces of UNICEF. They are selected from prominent figures in music, sports, film and related fields. Their major objective is to "raise awareness and mobilize support, helping UNICEF to reach the most disadvantaged children and adolescents with lifesaving

SIX

help and hope".[207] In this mission of international service, Rose shares space with celebrities such as Katy Perry, Leo Messi, Danny Glover and Jackie Chan. Rose's readily recognizable identity on the global stage has positioned her to function effectively as an activist on behalf of the most vulnerable in communities around the world.

Over the course of Calypso Rose's career, spanning more than six decades, she has amassed a tidy fortune. This was not always the case. In the 1960s, when she first started singing in the tents in Trinidad, Rose made between $100 and $250 in local currency per week. By 1978, the year she won the Road March, her weekly income had reached $3,000.[208] Even in the years when her earnings were lean, Rose created a legacy as a patron of charitable causes. In 1976, when Rose won the National Calypso Queen Competition of Trinidad and Tobago for the third time in a row, she donated $200 to a children's home in the country. The cash prize offered for first place in the competition totalled $1,500. The soft drink company with headquarters in San Fernando, S.M. Jaleel, sponsored the prize.[209] Her second Road March cash prize of $3,000 won in 1978 with the tune "Come Leh We Jam" was also donated to charity. Rose shared the modest sum among three hospitals in Port of Spain, San Fernando and Tobago.[210] One of the reasons Rose has been honoured by the government and people of Liberia is that in the 1980s, she allocated proceeds from her concerts to build a primary school in Liberia, which now bears her name.[211] To raise funds for the Lady Hochoy Home for Handicapped Children with branches in Gasparillo, Cocorite and Arima in Trinidad, in 1988, Rose performed at the Commonwealth Institute in London and gave part of the proceeds to the Home and part to purchase equipment for the office of the London High Commission in Trinidad and Tobago.[212] Rose has also entered into arrangements with children's institutions in Jamaica, Belize and Haiti to provide annual funding for their causes on a first-come, first-served basis.[213] Perhaps her most selfless and significant donation to date has been the entrusting of her entire archive from the beginning of her career to the present to the Tobago House of Assembly. It is her expressed wish that generations of researchers and other visitors to the Icons of Tobago Museum, opened in 2019 and located at Fort George in Tobago, will have access to her papers. Rose also donated all of her awards to the Icons of Tobago Museum, including the prestigious Victoires de la Musique Award.[214] In 2024, on one of her many visits to her island home, Tobago, Rose made an undisclosed financial contribution to the Tobago Regional Health Authority's Dialysis Unit at the Scarborough Health Centre. Dr Faith B. Yisrael, secretary of health, wellness and social protection, received the cheque on behalf of the medical department. Rose explained that she was motivated by her desire to give back to Tobago and by the island's kidney foundation, through which kidney patients like herself could receive treatment.[215] Rose has been magnanimous in sharing her resources.

Conclusion

The life experiences of McCartha Linda Monica Sandy-Lewis have been compelling, and her responses to them have been

SIX

phenomenal. From the time of her birth in 1940 to the present, 2026, Rose has consistently demonstrated a battle-ready disposition in the face of the many challenges she has encountered during the eighty-five years she has lived on this earth. She overcame the obscurity of her birth to take centre stage in numerous prominent places in the world. She entered the calypso entertainment industry as a woman, only to emerge as one of the strongest in her chosen field. She defied religious and sexual critics by insisting that Christianity is analogous to and not antagonistic to both calypso music and homosexuality. Refusing to lie down when one illness after another plagued her body, she has taken her place among cancer survivors and others who have successfully fought off debilitating diseases. Not even age has succeeded in conquering Calypso Rose, for her latter years as a calypsonian have been greater than her former. She has been widely acclaimed, repeatedly honoured and has left a legacy of great magnanimity. Rose is a calypsonian extraordinaire, and there has been none like her before nor since.

NOTES

1. Brown, "Calypso Rose: I Am Here to Tell Women Don't Be Afraid."
2. Fanfair, "Calypso Rose Ageing Well Like Old Wine."
3. Fulani, *Archipelagos of Sound*, 246.
4. Staff Writer, *Trinidad Express*, 22 September 2000, 8.
5. Kefim, "Calypso Rose: My Meetings with the Undisputed Queen of Calypso."
6. John, "The Petals Have Not Withered."
7. Lee, "A Rose in Name and Nature," B1.
8. Ibid.
9. Brown, "Calypso Rose."
10. Lakhan, "An Interview with Calypso Rose."
11. Lee, "A Rose in Name and Nature," B1.
12. See "Calypso Rose – Back to Africa."
13. Lakhan, "An Interview with Calypso Rose."
14. McCallister, "Career of Singing Calypso Rose."
15. Matthews, "Pursuing Freedom," 101–12.
16. See "Calypso Rose: Queen of the Calypso World."
17. John, "The Petals Have Not Withered."
18. See "Calypso Rose: Queen of the Calypso World."
19. Brown, "Calypso Rose."
20. McCallister, "Career of Singing Calypso Rose."

NOTES

21. Fraser, "The Legacy of Calypso Rose."
22. Staff Writer, "Calypso Revues: A Little Nostalgia."
23. Ottley, *Women in Calypso*, 6.
24. Daniell, "Calypso Showcase: Calypso Rose."
25. See "Build Monument in Scarborough – Rose," B3.
26. Ottley, *Women in Calypso*, 2.
27. Lorraine 1606, "Calypso Rose: Lioness of the Jungle Trailer."
28. Rampersad, "Calypso Rose – On the Road Again," 1998, 7.
29. See "Constable Rose."
30. Daniell, "Calypso Showcase: Calypso Rose."
31. City of New York Police Department certificate awarded to Linda McCartha Sandy-Lewis.
32. Fanfair, "Ageing Well Like Old Wine."
33. See "How to Become a Police Auxiliary Officer."
34. Rampersad, "Calypso Rose – On the Road Again," 7.
35. Staff Writer, *Trinidad Express*, 22 September 2000, 8.
36. *MyBelize.Net*, "The Name of the Rose Is Calypso."
37. Daniell, "Calypso Showcase: Calypso Rose."
38. Rampersad, "Calypso Rose for NAPA Concert."
39. Peck, "This 78-Year-Old Artist Just Became Coachella's Oldest Performer."
40. Gosine, "Rose in France."
41. *Loop News*, "Calypso Rose Wins French Grammy."
42. *VP Voice*, "Calypso Rose from Grant to Grammy," 2017.
43. See "Tribute to Legendary Calypso Rose."
44. Ottley, *Women in Calypso*, 15.
45. Lee, "A Rose in Name and Nature," B1.
46. Campbell, "In Calypso and Soca: Woman Is Boss."
47. *SKN News*, "The First Woman in Trinidad and Tobago to Take the Stage in a Calypso Tent?"
48. Lee, "A Rose in Name and Nature," B2.
49. *Repeating Islands*, "Artist Profiles: Calypso Rose."

NOTES

50. Anderson, "Calypso Rose," 172.
51. Powell, "Calypso Rose: Fire in Me Wire."
52. Batzen, "Calypso Rose Fire in Me Wire Live at Petit Bain Paris May 26, 2012."
53. Sander and Springer, "Every Trinidad Road March."
54. Powell, "Calypso Rose: Fire in Me Wire."
55. Loubon, "Fire in Me Wire," 7.
56. Fraser, "The Legacy of Calypso Rose."
57. Dean, "Calypso as a Vehicle for Political Commentary."
58. Meschino, "78-Year-Old Caribbean Trailblazer Calypso Rose."
59. Daniell, "The Best of Calypso Rose."
60. Healy, "Anaparima Calling."
61. Fraser, "The Legacy of Calypso Rose."
62. Caribbean Insight Television, "Rising Stars of Women Road March."
63. Anderson, "Calypso Rose," 172.
64. Daniell, "The Best of Calypso Rose."
65. Bishop, "Composer of 'Her Majesty' Dies at 75," 3.
66. Troughton, "Carnival Queen Calypso Rose Interviewed."
67. Healy, "The Era of Chalkdust."
68. Brown, "Singing Francine: The Original Parang Soca Queen."
69. Rampersad, "Rose Is Boss," 27–28.
70. Lewis, "One Is Enough."
71. Brown, "Calypso Rose."
72. See "Calypso Rose, 'Leave Me Alone.'"
73. See "Calypso Rose, 'A Man Is a Man.'"
74. See "Calypso Rose, 'Do Dem Back.'"
75. Austin, "Understanding Calypso Content," 80.
76. See "What She Want."
77. See "Calypso Rose on the BBC."
78. See "Me Doh Want No Married Man."
79. Bolles, "Making It Work in the English-Speaking Caribbean," 12.

NOTES

80. See "Wha She Go Do."
81. Quan, "Walter's Big Adventure," 1.
82. See "Sideman Sweet."
83. See "Don't Touch Me."
84. See "Calypso Rose: The Woman behind the Music."
85. See "Solomon."
86. Calixte, 14.
87. Ramm, "The Subversive Power of Calypso Music."
88. John, "The Petals Have Not Withered."
89. See "Calypso Rose: Queen of the Calypso World."
90. *Caribbean National Weekly*, "Calypso Rose: Queen of the Road."
91. Rampersad, "Rose Is Boss," 27–28.
92. See "Turn on the Pressure."
93. See "Have Mercy."
94. See John, "The Petals Have Not Withered."
95. See "No Madam."
96. Hillier, "Calypso Rose: The Calypso Queen."
97. Adkins, 216.
98. See "Gunplay on D'Parkway."
99. Hevesi, "Founders of the Labour Day Parade."
100. See "Jump Up for Independence."
101. See "Ezekiel Coming."
102. See "They Say I Reign Too Long."
103. Caribbean Insight Television, "Calypso Rose: Queen of the Calypso World."
104. Daniell, "Calypso Showcase: Calypso Rose."
105. See "Calypso Rose: Queen of the Calypso World."
106. Fulani, *Archipelagos of Sound*, 257.
107. John, "The Petals Have Not Withered."
108. Lee, "A Rose in Name and Nature," B1.
109. Fulani, *Archipelagos of Sound*, 257–258.
110. Zisman, "Calypso Rose: Interview Vidéo."

NOTES

111. Campbell, "Calypso Rose Musical."
112. Hillier, "Calypso Rose: The Calypso Queen."
113. Dyer, "Calypso Rose Is the 77-Year-Old Patron Saint of Women Who Love to Fete."
114. Daniell, "Calypso Showcase: Calypso Rose."
115. Rohlehr, *A Scuffling of Islands*, 237–38; see also Ottley, *Women in Calypso*, 5.
116. Davies Boyce, "Woman Is a Nation."
117. Newsday Reporter, "Calypso Rose Musical."
118. Caribbean Insight Television, "Queen of the Calypso World."
119. Romero, "Artist Profiles: Calypso Rose."
120. See *MyCaribNews*, "Musical on Calypso Rose: A Story to Be Told."
121. Fulani, *Archipelagos of Sound*, 258.
122. Spenser, "A Rose Among Thorns."
123. Surtee, "Calypso Rose: An Icon for the Caribbean LGBT Community."
124. Campbell, "Calypso Rose Musical."
125. *Chutney Pride*, "Exclusive Coming Out Interview with Calypso Rose."
126. Surtee, "Icon for the Caribbean LGBT Community."
127. Fanfair, "Ageing Well Like Old Wine."
128. Morgan, "Calypso Rose: Queen of the World."
129. MusicTT, "Calypso Rose Shares Her Experiences."
130. John, "The Petals Have Not Withered."
131. MusicTT, "Calypso Rose Shares Her Experiences."
132. Emrit, "Calypso Rose."
133. Hillier, "The Calypso Queen."
134. Daniell, "Calypso Showcase: Calypso Rose."
135. Fanfair, "Ageing Well Like Old Wine."
136. Lee, "A Rose in Name and Nature," B2.
137. Staff Writer, *Trinidad Express*, 22 September, 8.
138. John, "The Petals Have Not Withered."

NOTES

139. MusicTT, "Calypso Rose Shares Her Experiences."
140. Ibid.
141. Clark, "Calypso Rose: A Breast Cancer Survivor's Melody."
142. Aspiring Minds Foundation, "Calypso Rose."
143. Duke-Westfield, "Her Majesty Conquers Cancer," section 2.
144. Dyer, "Patron Saint of Women Who Love to Fete."
145. *Jamaica Gleaner*, "Aging with Dignity."
146. John, "The Petals Have Not Withered."
147. Evans, "Calypso Rose Interview at Globalquerque."
148. Joseph, "I'm Still Batting, Says Rose."
149. Ibid.
150. Saxberg, "Calypso Rose: Blazing a Trail for Women in Music."
151. Meschino, "78-Year-Old Caribbean Trailblazer Calypso Rose."
152. Doodnath, "Calypso Rose, up and about after Hospital Visit."
153. See "Paying Tribute to Calypso Rose."
154. Peck, "Coachella's Oldest Performer."
155. Spark, "I Am Alive and in Good Health."
156. Webb, "Calypso Rose: I Will Be Home for Tobago Carnival."
157. Green, "Calypso Rose Cancels Summer Tour."
158. See "Kamalo Deen – Director of 'Bacchanal Time.'"
159. Pempalah Productions, "Bacchanal Time – The Movie", 2025.
160. TTT Live Online, "One Hand Don't Clap."
161. Regent Theatre Video, "One Hand Don't Clap with Poster."
162. IMZ International Music+Music Media, "World Music Films on Tour."
163. Caribbean Tales Worldwide, "Dirty Jim's Calypso Jam."
164. See "Calypso Dreams Pt 1."
165. West Indian Connection, "Calypso Dreams documentary DVD."
166. Persad, "Documentary on Calypso Rose," 8.
167. "Rose for Toronto Film Festival," 9.
168. African Film Festival New Zealand, "Calypso Rose Lioness of the Jungle Trailer."

NOTES

169. Ibid.
170. University of Toronto, "Queen of the Road: The Calypso Rose Musical."
171. Campbell, "Calypso Rose Musical."
172. See *Trinidad and Tobago's 'Queen': Calypso Rose*.
173. Brown, "Calypso Rose."
174. Fanfair, "Ageing Well Like Old Wine."
175. Kefim, "Undisputed Queen of Calypso."
176. Mondezie, "Being Frank Spektakula Leads the Way."
177. Romero, "Artiste Profiles: Calypso Rose."
178. Darville, "Calypso Rose Pulls Machel Montano."
179. Williams, "Large Up Premier: Calypso Rose+ Machel Montano Do It Again with 'Young Boy.'"
180. American Blues Scene Staff, "Calypso Rose Announces New Album 'Forever.'"
181. See "Calypso Rose Announces New Album 'Forever' with 'Watina' Music Video."
182. Romero, "Artist Profiles: Calypso Rose."
183. Ali, "Calypso Rose Receives Trinidad's Highest Honor."
184. Ali, "Chalkdust Awarded T&T Highest Award."
185. Emrit, "Calypso Rose."
186. Tobago House of Assembly, "Calypso Rose Honoured by the THA."
187. Fraser, "Calypso Rose 'Thankful' to THA."
188. *Jamaica Observer*, "CAL Dedicates Jets to Honour Calypso Rose."
189. *UWI Today*, "Citation: McCartha Linda Sandy-Lewis."
190. Fraser, "The Legacy of Calypso Rose."
191. Loubon, "Fire in Me Wire," 7.
192. Lakhan, "An Interview with Calypso Rose."
193. *UWI Today*, "Citation: McCartha Linda Sandy-Lewis."
194. Benjamin, "Calypso Rose 'Pepper Soup."
195. Aspiring Minds, "Calypso Rose."

NOTES

196. Mondezie, "Calypso Rose Drops New Album."
197. Aspiring Minds, "Calypso Rose."
198. Rampersad, "Calypso Rose for NAPA Concert."
199. Mondezie, "Calypso Rose Drops New Album."
200. John, "The Petals Have Not Withered."
201. Bowman, "Rose Gets Keys to City," 12.
202. CNEWS, "Calypso Rose Gets Keys to San Fernando."
203. John, "The Petals Have Not Withered."
204. Fanfair, "Ageing Well Like Old Wine."
205. *UWI Today*, "Citation: McCartha Linda Sandy-Lewis."
206. Greene-Dewasmes, "Afro Wave, 2024."
207. See "UNICEF Goodwill Ambassadors."
208. Otley, *Women in Calypso*, 21.
209. Alleyne, "Rose Does It Again," 12.
210. Rampersad, "Calypso Rose on the Road," 7.
211. Ibid.
212. Staff Writer, "Assam Honours Calypso Rose," 9.
213. Rampersad, "Calypso Rose on the Road," 7.
214. Greaves, "Icons of Tobago Museum."
215. Newsday Reporter, "Calypso Rose Donated to Tobago Dialysis Unit."

BIBLIOGRAPHY

African Film Festival New Zealand. "*Calypso Rose: Lioness of the Jungle* Trailer." YouTube video, 1 March 2016. https://www.youtube.com/watch?v=wSyncTYl6Wo. Accessed 28 June 2024.

Ali, Azad. "Calypso Rose Receives Trinidad's Highest Honor." *Caribbean Life*, 3 October 2017. https://www.caribbeanlife.com/calypso-rose-receives-trinidads-highest-honor/. Accessed 2 July 2024.

Ali, Azad. "Chalkdust Awarded T&T's Highest Honor." *Caribbean Life*, 26 September 2016. https://www.caribbeanlife.com/chalkdust-awarded-tts-highest-honor/. Accessed 2 July 2024.

Alleyne, John. "Rose Does It Again." *Trinidad Evening News*, 12 February 1976, 12.

American Blues Scene Staff. "Calypso Rose Announces New Album *Forever*." *American Blues Scene*, 24 May 2022. https://www.americanbluesscene.com/2022/05/calypso-rose-announces-new-album-forever/. Accessed 5 May 2025.

Anderson, Keith. "Calypso Rose." In *The Ins and Outs of Trinidad and Tobago*, 10th ed. Port of Spain: Prospect Press, 2010.

Aspiring Minds Foundation. "Calypso Rose." Aspiring Minds Trinidad and Tobago. https://www.aspiringmindstandt.com/calypso-rose. Accessed 17 June 2024.

Benjamin, Gentle. "G.B.T.V. Archives 1991: Calypso Rose 'Pepper

Soup.'" YouTube video, 15 July 2012. https://www.youtube.com/watch?v=p5VY55ykYTI. Accessed 11 July 2024.

Bishop, Verdel. "Composer of 'Her Majesty' Dies at 75." *Trinidad Express*, 3 April 2013, 3.

Bolles, Lynn A. "Making It Work in the English-Speaking Caribbean: Women as Mothers, Providers, and Leaders." Paper presented at the Latin American Studies Association Conference, 1998. http://lasa.international.pitt.edu/LASA98/Bolles.pdf. Accessed 26 August 2013.

Bowman, Wayne. "Rose Gets Keys to City." *Trinidad Guardian*, 21 January 2003, 12.

Brown, Helen. "Calypso Rose: 'I Am Here to Tell Women, Don't Be Afraid.'" *The Independent*, 6 April 2020. https://www.independent.co.uk/arts-entertainment/music/features/calypso-rose-interview-b1015452.html. Accessed 18 June 2024.

Brown, Miguel. "Singing Francine: The Original Parang Soca Queen." *CatholicTT*, 10 January 2023. https://catholictt.org/2023/01/10/singing-francine-the-original-parang-soca-queen/. Accessed 31 March 2025.

Campbell, Nigel. "Women in Calypso: History and Influence." *iRADIO.tt Blog + Journal*, 1 November 2024. https://iradio.tt/women-in-calypso-history-and-influence/. Accessed 31 March 2025.

Campbell, Nigel. "Calypso Rose Musical: A Story for the World to Discover." *Trinidad and Tobago Newsday*, 15 May 2024. https://newsday.co.tt/2024/05/15/calypso-rose-musical-a-story-for-the-world-to-discover/. Accessed 2 July 2024.

Caribbean Insight Television. "Calypso Rose: Queen of the Calypso World." YouTube video, 9 July 2016. https://www.youtube.com/watch?v=Z9YsdLx6v9c. Accessed 19 June 2024.

———. "Rising Stars of Women Road March: Calypso Rose, Sanell Dempster, Fay-Ann Lyons and Patrice Roberts." YouTube video, 9 June 2023. https://www.youtube.com/watch?v=F-VLZWKhfo. Accessed 20 June 2024.

———. "Rose: The Calypso Queen Who Dared to Dream." YouTube video. https://www.youtube.com/watch?v=DPpSbu-s1Wo. Accessed 19 February 2025.

Clark, Michele. "Calypso Rose: A Breast Cancer Survivor's Melody of Courage and Advocacy." *LinkedIn*, 22 February 2024. https://www.linkedin.com/pulse/calypso-rose-breast-cancer-survivors-melody-courage-advocacy. Accessed 17 June 2024.

CNEWS. "Calypso Rose Gets Keys to San Fernando." YouTube video, 7 March 2017. https://www.youtube.com/watch?v=h-PwTOZ1Hmo. Accessed 9 July 2024.

Daniell, Alvin. "Calypso Rose – *The Best of Calypso Rose*." *Discogs*, 19 March 2012. https://www.discogs.com/release. Accessed 20 June 2024.

———. "Calypso Showcase: Calypso Rose." YouTube video, 9 January 2022. https://www.youtube.com/watch?v=aVkEdmM-cbE. Accessed 30 January 2025. YouTube

Darville, Jordan. "Calypso Rose Pulls Machel Montano for Her 'Leave Me Alone' Music Video." *The Fader*, 15 December 2016. https://www.thefader.com/2016/12/15/calypso-rose-machel-montano-for-her-leave-me-alone-music-video. Accessed 9 May 2025.

Davies Boyce, Carole. "Woman Is a Nation Woman: Caribbean Oral Literature." In *Out of the Kumbla: Caribbean Women and Literature*, edited by Carole Boyce Davies and Elaine Savory Fido, 103–121. Trenton, NJ: Africa World Press, 1983.

Dean, Daryl. *Calypso as a Vehicle for Political Commentary: An Endangered Musical Species*. Unpublished MA thesis, Carleton University, Ottawa, Ontario, 2015, 103. https://www.collectionscanada.gc.ca/obj/thesescanada/vol2/002.PDF. Accessed 10 August 2024.

Doodnath, Alina. "Calypso Rose, Up and About after Hospital Visit." *Loop News*, 2025. https://www.loopnews.com/content/calypso-rose-up-and-about-after-hospital-visit/. Accessed 24 April 2025.

Duke-Westfield, Nicole. "Her Majesty Conquers Cancer: Rose Comes Back with Fire." *Trinidad Express*, 23 January 1998, Section 2.

Dyer, Deidre. "Calypso Rose Is the 77-Year-Old Patron Saint of Women Who Love to Fete." *The Fader*, 23 August 2017. https://www.thefader.com/2017/08/23/calypso-rose-patron-saint-interview. Accessed 18 June 2024.

Emrit, Ronald. "Calypso Rose." *Best of Trinidad*. https://www.bestoftrinidad.com/calypso/rose.html. Accessed 18 June 2024.

Evans, Paul. "Calypso Rose Interview at Globalquerque 2014." YouTube video, 25 September 2014. https://www.youtube.com/watch?v=2ZOBGwJwAtw. Accessed 19 June 2024. YouTube

Fanfair, Ron. "Calypso Rose Ageing Well Like Old Wine." *Ron Fanfair's blog*, 31 January 2018. https://ronfanfair.wordpress.com/2018/01/31/calypso-rose-ageing-well-like-old-wine/. Accessed 11 July 2024.

Fraser, Fayola. "The Legacy of Calypso Rose." *CNC3*, 7 April 2024. https://www.cnc3.co.tt/the-legacy-of-calypso-rose/. Accessed 20 June 2024.

Fraser, Marissa. "Calypso Rose 'Thankful' to THA as Street Renamed in Her Honour." *Trinidad and Tobago Newsday*, 26 October 2024. https://newsday.co.tt/2024/10/26/calypso-rose-thankful-to-tha-as-street-renamed-in-her-honour/. Accessed 27 July 2025.

Fulani, Ifeona, ed. *Archipelagos of Sound: Transnational Caribbean Women and Music*. Kingston: University of the West Indies Press, 2012.

Greaves, Deborah. "Icons of Tobago Museum Opens." *Trinidad and Tobago Newsday*, 19 March 2019. https://newsday.co.tt/2019/03/19/icons-of-tobago-museum-opens/. Accessed 27 July 2025.

Greene-Dewasmes, Ginelle. "Afro Wave: How the Arts Can Empower African and Afro-Diaspora Nations in Global Discourse." *World Economic Forum*, 24 February 2024. https://www.weforum.org/stories/2024/02/how-the-arts-can-empower-african-and-afro-diaspora-nations-in-global-discourse/. Accessed 11 July 2024.

Gosine, Andil. "Rose in France." In *A Rose Among Thorns: Calypso Rose—Life, Music and Impact*. YouTube video. https://www.youtube.com/watch?v=EuYMmSABl80. Accessed 26 March 2025.

BIBLIOGRAPHY

Green, Patrick. "Calypso Rose Cancels Summer Tour." *Caribbean National Weekly (CNW Network)*, 24 February 2022. https://www.caribbeannationalweekly.com/entertainment/calypso-rose-cancels-summer-tour/. Accessed 18 June 2024.

Healy, Dara. "The Era of Chalkdust." *Trinidad and Tobago Newsday*, 28 September 2019. https://newsday.co.tt/2019/09/28/the-era-of-chalkdust/. Accessed 31 March 2025.

Healy, Dara. "Anaparima Calling." *Trinidad and Tobago Newsday*, 25 August 2018. https://newsday.co.tt/2018/08/25/anaparima-calling/. Accessed 20 June 2024.

Hevesi, Dennis. "Carlos Lezama, One of the Founders of the Labor Day Parade." *The New York Times*, 2017. https://www.nytimes.com/2017/12/26/obituaries/carlos-lezama-dead.html. Accessed 31 March 2025.

Hillier, Tony. "The Calypso Queen." *World Music Central*, 2 September 2011. http://worldmusiccentral.org/2011/09/02/the-calypso-queen/. Accessed 18 June 2013.

Jamaica Gleaner. "Ageing with Dignity: No Slowing Down for Calypso Rose at 78." 10 February 2019. https://jamaica-gleaner.com/article/entertainment/20190210/ageing-dignity-no-slowing-down-calypso-rose-78. Accessed 17 June 2024.

John, Deborah. "Calypso Rose: The Petals Have Not Withered." *Trinidad and Tobago News*, 26 September 2003. https://www.trinidadandtobagonews.com/John.html. Accessed 17 June 2024.

Joseph, Terry. "I'm Still Batting, Says Rose." *Trinicentre.net*, 18 March 2001. https://www.trinicentre.net/ilevel/2001/terry-j-im-still-batting-says-rose/. Accessed 17 June 2024.

Kefim, Ras. "Calypso Rose: My Meetings with the Undisputed Queen of Calypso." *Black Star News*. https://blackstarnews.com/article/calypso-rose-my-meetings-undisputed-queen-calypso/. Accessed 11 July 2024.

Lakhan, Anu. "An Interview with Calypso Rose." *Explore Parts Unknown*,

14 June 2017. https://explorepartsunknown.com/an-interview-with-calypso-rose/. Accessed 9 July 2024.

Lee, Simon. "A Rose in Name and Nature." *Trinidad Guardian*, 11 May 2009, B1–B2.

Lewis, Arthur. "One Is Enough." *Trinidad Express*, 8 January 1979.

Loop News. "Calypso Rose Wins French Grammy." 10 February 2017. https://www.loopnews.com/content/calypso-rose-wins-french-grammy/. Accessed 31 March 2025.

Loubon, Michelle. "Fire in Me Wire." *Trinidad Guardian*, 2 February 2023, 7.

Matthews, Gelien. "Pursuing Freedom: Enslaved Revolts in Trinidad and Tobago." In *Foundation Readings on the History of Trinidad and Tobago*, edited by Sandra John, 101–12. Port of Spain: Ministry of Education, Government of the Republic of Trinidad and Tobago, 2017.

McCallister, Jared. "Career of Singer Calypso Rose Subject of AfroPoP Documentary Series on WORLD." *New York Daily News*, 5 February 2012, updated 10 January 2019. https://www.nydailynews.com/2012/02/05/career-of-singer-calyso-rose-subject-of-afropop-documentary-series-on-world/. Accessed 25 March 2025.

Meschino, Patricia. "78-Year-Old Caribbean Trailblazer Calypso Rose on Her History-Making Coachella Gig." *Billboard*, 4 October 2019. https://www.billboard.com/music/music-news/calypso-rose-coachella-interview-8530972/. Accessed 20 June 2024.

Mondezie, Michael. "Being Frank: Spektakula Leads the Way for Acceptance of Local Music." *Trinidad Express*, https://trinidadexpress.com/features/being-frank/article_c0053266-2024-11e8-a7c7-5fd3dcbbd083.html. Accessed 15 October 2024.

———. "Calypso Rose Drops New Album on August 26." *Trinidad Express*, 4 June 2022. https://trinidadexpress.com/features/local/now-forever/article_3a5a0d36-e3d1-11ec-bde3-3b9dbaf7c9c4.html. Accessed 9 July 2024.

Morgan, Maicaiah. "Calypso Rose: Queen of the World." *Caribbean*

National Weekly (CNW Network), 21 August 2022. https://www.caribbeannationalweekly.com/entertainment/calypso-rose-queen-of-the-world/. Accessed 17 June 2024.

MusicTT. "Calypso Rose Shares Her Experiences." YouTube video, 2 November 2017. https://www.youtube.com/watch?v=8x8zP2nZ9iQ. Accessed 19 June 2024.

MyCaribNews. "Musical on Calypso Rose: A Story to Be Told." 20 November 2020. https://nycaribnews.com/musical-on-calypso-rose-a-story-to-be-told/. Accessed 2 April 2025.

Newsday Reporter. "Calypso Rose Donates to Tobago Dialysis Unit." *Trinidad and Tobago Newsday*, 29 October 2024. https://newsday.co.tt/2024/10/29/calypso-rose-donates-to-trha-dialysis-unit/. Accessed 24 July 2025.

———. "Calypso Rose Musical: A Story for the World to Discover." *Trinidad and Tobago Newsday*, 15 May 2024. https://newsday.co.tt/2024/05/15/calypso-rose-musical-a-story-for-the-world-to-discover/. Accessed 19 June 2024.

Ottley, C. R. *Women in Calypso, Part 1*. Arima, Trinidad: Self-published, 1992.

Peck, Patrice. "This 78-Year-Old Artist Just Became Coachella's Oldest Performer—But She's Been Making History Since 1955." *BuzzFeed*, 16 April 2019. https://www.buzzfeed.com/patricepeck/calypso-rose-coachella-oldest-performer-trinidad. Accessed 10 May 2025.

Pempelah Productions. "*Bacchanal Time* – The Movie." Pempelah Productions. https://pempelahproductions.com/bacchanal-time-the-movie/. Accessed 1 April 2025.

Persad, Seeta. "Documentary on Calypso Rose to Be Released." *Trinidad Express*, 22 July 2009, 8.

Powell, Azizi. "Calypso Rose: Fire in Me Wire." *Pancocojams*, 5 October 2013. https://pancocojams.blogspot.com/2013/10/calypso-rose-fire-in-me-wire.html. Accessed 20 June 2024.

Quan, Tracy. "Walter's Big Adventure: A Review of *Killing Johnny Fry: A

Sexistential Novel." January Magazine. http://www.januarymagazine.com. Accessed 13 June 2013.

Ramm, Benjamin. "The Subversive Power of Calypso Music." *BBC Culture*, 11 October 2017. https://www.bbc.com/culture/article/20171011-the-subversive-power-of-calypso-music. Accessed 6 August 2024.

Rampersad, Joan. "Calypso Rose for NAPA Concert." *Trinidad and Tobago Newsday*, 27 January 2018. https://newsday.co.tt/2018/01/27/calypso-rose-for-napa-concert/. Accessed 10 May 2025.

Rampersad, Kris. "Calypso Rose – On the Road Again." *Trinidad Sunday Guardian*, 25 January 1998, 7.

Rampersad, Sheila. "Rose Is Boss." *Trinidad Express*, 30 July 1993, 27–28.

Regent Theatre Video. "One Hand Don't Clap: Trailer with Poster." YouTube video, 15 October 2023. https://www.youtube.com/watch?v=KZ9qvQZ3k1I. Accessed 1 July 2024.

Repeating Islands. "Artist Profiles: Calypso Rose." 20 January 2020. https://repeatingislands.com/2020/01/20/artist-profiles-calypso-rose/. Accessed 20 June 2024.

Rohlehr, Gordon. *A Scuffling of Islands: Essays on Calypso*. San Juan, Trinidad: Lexicon Trinidad Ltd., 2004.

Romero, Angel. "Artist Profiles: Calypso Rose." *World Music Central*, 16 January 2017. https://worldmusiccentral.org/2017/01/16/artist-profiles-calypso-rose/. Accessed 19 June 2024.

Sander, Phillip, and Atillah Springer. "Every Trinidad Road March Ever—and Our Top Ten." *Caribbean Beat*, no. 149 (January/February 2018). https://www.caribbean-beat.com/issue-149/ten-for-the-road. Accessed 20 June 2024.

Saxberg, Lynn. "Calypso Rose: Blazing a Trail for Women in Music." *Ottawa Citizen*, 18 January 2018. https://ottawacitizen.com/entertainment/music/calypso-rose-blazing-a-trail-for-women-in-music. Accessed 18 June 2024.

SKN News. "Do You Know Who Was the First Woman in Trinidad and

Tobago to Take the Stage in a Calypso Tent?" 7 October 2021. https://sknnews.com/featured/do-you-know-who-was-the-first-woman-in-trinidad-and-tobago-to-take-the-stage-in-a-calypso-tent/. Accessed 31 March 2024.

Spark, Stephen. "Calypso Rose: 'I Am Alive and in Good Health.'" *Soca News*, 17 October 2022. https://soca-news.com/2022/10/17/calypso-rose-i-am-alive-and-in-good-health/. Accessed 17 June 2024.

Spenser, Rhoma. "*A Rose Among Thorns: Calypso Rose—Life, Music and Impact.*" YouTube video. https://www.youtube.com/watch?v=EuYMmSABl8o. Accessed 30 August 2024.

Staff Writer. "Calypso Revues: A Little Nostalgia, A Lot of Song." *St Thomas Source*, 21 April 2002. https://stthomassource.com/content/2002/04/21/calypso-revues-a-little-nostalgia-a-lot-of-song/. Accessed 31 March 2025.

Staff Writer. "Assam Honours Calypso Rose." *Trinidad Guardian*, 9 July 1988, 9.

Surtee, Joshua. "Calypso Rose: An Icon for the Caribbean LGBT Community." *Trinidad and Tobago Newsday*, 13 January 2019. https://newsday.co.tt/2019/01/13/calypso-rose-an-icon-for-the-caribbean-lgbt-community/. Accessed 2 July 2024.

Tobago House of Assembly. "Calypso Rose Honoured by the THA." 19 August 2016. https://tha.gov.tt/calypso-rose-honoured-by-the-tha/. Accessed 4 July 2024.

Troughton, Richie. "Watch: Carnival Queen Calypso Rose Interviewed." *The Quietus*, 21 April 2016. https://thequietus.com/articles/20238-calypso-rose-interview. Accessed 24 June 2024.

TTT Live Online. "*One Hand Don't Clap*: Documentary Featuring Lord Kitchener." YouTube video, 18 April 2022. https://www.youtube.com/watch?v=6vYqG9XxwoY. Accessed 1 July 2024.

University of Toronto. "*Queen of the Road: The Calypso Rose Musical.*" Hart House Theatre, University of Toronto. https://harthouse.ca/theatre/queen-of-the-road-the-calypso-rose-musical/. Accessed 2 July 2024.

UWI Today. "Citation: McCartha Linda Sandy-Lewis, Degree of Doctor of Letters (DLL)." 14 December 2014. https://uwitoday.uwi.edu/citation-mccartha-linda-sandy-lewis-degree-doctor-letters-dll. Accessed 5 July 2024.

VP Voice. "Calypso Rose: From Grant to Grammy." 8 May 2017. https://thevoiceslu.com/2017/05/calypso-rose-grant-grammy/. Accessed 25 April 2025.

Webb, Yvonne. "Calypso Rose: I Will Be Home for Tobago Carnival." *Trinidad and Tobago Newsday*, 15 September 2022. https://newsday.co.tt/2022/09/15/calypso-rose-i-will-be-home-for-tobago-carnival/. Accessed 17 June 2024.

Williams, Tishanna. "LargeUp Premier: Calypso Rose + Machel Montano Do It Again with 'Young Boy.'" *LargeUp*, 31 December 2018. https://www.largeup.com/2018/12/31/calypso-rose-machel-montano-young-boy/. Accessed 9 May 2025.

Zisman, Marc. "Calypso Rose: Interview vidéo." YouTube video (Qobuz), 25 May 2016. https://www.youtube.com/watch?v=QmZPZkRrKp8. Accessed 19 June 2024.

ACKNOWLEDGEMENTS

In writing this book, staff of the National Library, Icons of Tobago Museum and the National Archives of Trinidad and Tobago assisted me in accessing sources. Thank you. Special thanks to Miguel Brown and Dr Rudolph Ottley for their valuable support. I also appreciate Richard Holder for graciously allowing me to use his photograph of Calypso Rose. Above all, I thank God for the opportunity to pursue and complete this research.

www.ingramcontent.com/pod-product-compliance
Lightning Source LLC
LaVergne TN
LVHW041532070526
838199LV00046B/1629